THE STIGMATA OF FRANCIS OF ASSISI

New Studies
New Perspectives

THE STIGMATA OF FRANCIS OF ASSISI

New Studies
New Perspectives

Franciscan Institute Publications
The Franciscan Institute
St. Bonaventure, NY
2006

Copyright © 2006
Franciscan Institute Publications
Saint Bonaventure University
Saint Bonaventure, NY 14778

All rights reserved.
No part of this book may be reproduced or transmitted in any form or by any means, electronic or mechanical, without permission in writing from the publisher.

Cover Design: Roberta McKelvie, OSF
Credit: St. Francis Receiving the Stigmata (tempera on panel) by Gaddi, Taddeo (c.1300-66). Galleria dell' Accademia, Florence, Italy/ The Bridgeman Art Library Nationality / copyright status: Italian / out of copyright

Library of Congress Cataloging-in-Publication Data

The stigmata of Francis of Assisi : new studies, new perspectives.
   p. cm.
 ISBN 1-57659-140-9 (alk. paper)
 1. Francis, of Assisi, Saint, 1182-1226. 2. Stigmatization--Italy--Assisi--History. I. Dalarun, Jacques. Great secret of Francis. II. Cusato, Michael F. Of snakes and angels. III. Salvati, Carla. Camoscio.
 BX4700.F6S684 2006
 271'.302--dc22
                        2006008104

Printed in the United States of America
BookMasters
Ashland, Ohio

Contents

Preface	v
Jacques Dalarun The Great Secret of Francis	9

Michael F. Cusato
     Of Snakes and Angels:
     The Mystical Experience Behind the
     Stigmatization Narrative
	29

Carla Salvati
     The *Camoscio*: Relic of the Side Wound
     of Francis of Assisi, "Living Eucharist"
	79

List of Figures	101
Images in color	103

Editor's note:

Due to the inclusion of black and white images in the article by Carla Salvati, the notes have been included as endnotes rather than as footnotes. Color reproductions of the images follow the endnotes.

Preface

The stigmata of Francis of Assisi constitutes one of the more fascinating parts of the story of the Poor One in the many volumes that allow us to study his life both through his writings and the first storytellers of the Franciscan movement. Was the imprint of the wounds of Christ onto the body of Francis a hagiographic phenomenon, a re-writing of the story, or an imposition of later writers and artists? Is it acceptable to even raise that kind of question about something that is so deeply imbedded in the heart of the Francsican tradition? We hope that the essays in this volume challenge us to look at this part of our heritage with new eyes.

With the publication in 1993 of Chiara Frugoni's *Francesco: l'invenzione delle stimmate. Una storia per immagini e parole fino a Giotto ed a Bonaventura*, some scholars began to challenge the "reality" of the wounds of Francis, advancing the opinion that they were, for the most part, a theological concoction of Bonaventure that gained acceptance because of artistic representations of the event at La Verna in 1224. Over the last fifteen years many scholars have reexamined and reaffirmed the phenomenon we call the stigmata of Francis of Assisi. The essays contained in this volume are taken from two sessions held during the International Congress for Medieval Studies at Kalamazoo in May, 2005. They substantially complement and enrich current efforts to understand this high moment of Francis's spiritual experience, which Celano (*De miraculis*, 1-2) hailed as a "new and stupendous miracle" and the signature event of the "new man" that Francis was for his time.

The essays of Jacques Dalarun and Michael F. Cusato offer critical examinations of the historical event. Carla Salvati presents an excellent assessment of the importance of medieval devotion to the wounds of Christ while offering a fine study of the relics associated with the event. Taken together, they present contemporary interpretations of how the stigmata narration developed and its meaning for our time.

Is the stigmata a sign of God's approbation of the whole of Francis's life? Is it affirmation of his legitimacy as saint? Does it confirm him as founder of a major religious Order that still thrives in the 21st century? Or does it strengthen his role as prophet, challenging the boundaries of science and "realism" by calling forth deeper faith? Whether one views the stigmata of Francis as a "miracle" or not, the essays which follow must certainly challenge our perceptions and our perspectives.

Paul LaChance, O.F.M.
Catholic Theological Union
Chicago, IL

Roberta A. McKelvie, O.S.F.
St. Bonaventure University
Allegany, NY

THE GREAT SECRET OF FRANCIS

JACQUES DALARUN

Published in Italian in 1993, Chiara Frugoni's book *Francesco e l'invenzione delle stimmate* was immediately at the core of a lively debate.[1] The best specialists of Franciscan studies reviewed and discussed it. Among many others, we can cite at least Giovanni Miccoli's lecture published in 1997 and entitled *Considerazioni sulle stimmate*.[2]

I don't wish to extend the historiographical debate. Using the works of my predecessors rather than trying to contradict them, I would like to answer in a very positive way the simple questions: Had Francis wounds in his hands, his feet and his side? What did they look like? Where, when and how did he receive them? As usual, the only possible method one can follow is to examine the sources we have in the most likely chronological order.

During Francis's life, so before 1226, we have no mention of the fact. It's important to recall that Francis never spoke of his wounds in his writings. Whatever our conclusion may be, it will be impossible to say that Francis was a liar: a mute does not lie.

---

[1] Chiara Frugoni, *Francesco e l'invenzione delle stimmate: Una storia per parole e immagini fino a Bonaventura e Giotto* (Turin: Einaudi, 1993). See also Chiara Frugoni, *Vita di un uomo: Francesco d'Assisi* (Turin: Einaudi, 1995), trans. *Francis of Assisi: A Life* (New York: Continuum, 1998), 119-47. On the debate, see Jacques Dalarun, *La Malavventura di Francesco d'Assisi: Per un uso storico delle leggende francescane* (Milano: Edizioni Biblioteca Francescana, 1996); trans. *The Misadventure of Francis of Assisi: Toward a Historical Use of the Franciscan Legends* (St. Bonaventure, NY: Franciscan Institute Publications, 2002), 47-50. I thank warmly Timothy J. Johnson and Michael Cusato for their attentive reading and their valuable corrections and suggestions.

[2] Giovanni Miccoli, "Considerazioni sulle stimmate," in *Il fatto delle stimmate di S. Francesco* (Assisi: Edizioni Porziuncola, 1997), 13-39. I will often rely on this remarkable contribution. For a huge bibliographical review right before the publication of Frugoni's book, see Octavian Schmucki, *The Stigmata of St. Francis of Assisi: A Critical Investigation in the Light of the Thirteenth-Century Sources* (St. Bonaventure, NY: The Franciscan Institute, 1991), 7-69, 287-309 and 327-80. A very original perspective is offered by Richard C. Trexler, "The Stigmatized Body of Francis of Assisi: Conceived, Processed, Disappeared," in *Frömmigkeit im Mittelalter: Politisch-soziale Kontexte, visuelle Praxis, körperliche Ausdrucksformen*, Klaus Schreiner and Marc Müntz, eds. (Munich: Wilhem Fink Verlag, 2002), 463-97.

The first testimony–if the text is really authentic³–is the letter of Brother Elias, probably sent just after Francis's death: "And now, after telling you these things, I announce to you a great joy and the news of a miracle. Such a sign that has never been heard of from the dawn of time except in the Son of God, who is Christ the Lord. Not long before his death, our brother and father appeared crucified, bearing in his body the five wounds which are truly the stigmata of Christ. His hands and feet had, as it were, the openings of the nails and were pierced front and back revealing the scars and showing the nails' blackness. His side, moreover, seemed opened by a lance and often emitted blood."⁴

We learn four things: according to Elias, the fact is an absolute novelty;⁵ these five wounds are the "stigmata of Christ;" they appeared "not long before [Francis's] death;" they look like the holes of nails. But we can't know how they were produced.

The second testimony may be of Pope Gregory IX, in the bull *Mira circa nos* that he sends on July 19, 1228, in order to announce Francis's canonization.⁶ Indeed, I wonder if this passage is not a very discreet mention of Francis's wounds:

---

³See Felice Accrocca, "Un apocrifo la 'lettera enciclica di frate Elia sul transito di S. Francesco'?" *Collectanea Franciscana* 65 (1995): 473-509, and the reply of Miccoli, "Considerazioni," 16-20, with which I entirely agree.

⁴*Fontes Francescani*, Enrico Menestò and Stefano Brufani, eds. (Assisi: Edizioni Porziuncola, 1995), 255; *Francis of Assisi: Early Documents*, Regis J. Armstrong, J. A. Wayne Hellmann and William J. Short, eds., vol. 2, *The Founder* (New York: New City Press, 2000), 490. If I don't give other references, it means that I follow the Latin text of the *Fontes Franciscani* and the English text of *Francis of Assisi: Early Documents*, vols. 1, 2, 3, Regis J. Armstrong, J. A. Wayne Hellmann and William J. Short, eds. (New York: New City Press, 1999, 2000, 2001). Hereafter, *FAED*, with volume number. I have also adopted the abbreviations used in the American volumes.

⁵According to Trexler, "The Stigmatized Body," 487-88, the novelty announced by Elias is not the stigmata, but "the incredible change in Francis's body once he died." I only observe that, when Thomas of Celano in 1C 112-14 and then Bonaventure in LMj 15:1-4 jointly describe the beautiful corpse and the traces of the stigmata, they systematically present the second fact as more miraculous than the first one, which was a hagiographical *topos*.

⁶See Regis Armstrong, "*Mira circa nos*: Gregory's View of Saint Francis of Assisi," *Laurentianum* 25 (1984): 385-414, reprinted in *Greyfriars Review* 4 (1990): 75-100. See also Ruth Wolff, *Der heilige Franziskus in Schriften und Bildern des 13. Jahrhunderst* (Berlin: Mann, 1996), 37-59.

As he approached *the land of vision, on one of the mountains* that had been shown him – namely the height of faith – he offered as *a holocaust*[7] to the Lord his own flesh. As it previously deceived him, like Jepthah he offered this only-begotten daughter,[8] laying it on the fire of love, mortifying his flesh by hunger, thirst, cold, nakedness, fasting, and countless nights of prayer. When he had thus crucified his *flesh with its passions and desires*,[9] he was able to say with the Apostle: *It is no longer I who live, but Christ who lives in me*.[10] Truly, he no longer lived for himself, but rather for Christ, who died for our sins *and was raised for our justification*, so that we might no longer be enslaved to sin."[11]

According to the pope's presentation,[12] Francis's holocaust would have been the result of classically ascetic practices.[13]

The third testimony comes from the first *Life of Saint Francis* written by Thomas of Celano just after Francis's canonization in 1228. With the exception of a general announcement in the prologue of the second part of the legend,[14] we can distinguish three moments in which Thomas speaks of the stigmata.

The event happens "while [Francis] was staying in that hermitage called La Verna . . . two years prior to the time" of his death. "He saw in a vision of God a man, having six wings like a Seraph." And, further, "While he was unable to perceive anything clearly understandable from the vision, its newness very much pressed upon his heart. Signs of the nails began to appear on his hands and feet,

---

[7]Gen 22:2.
[8]Judges 11:34-35.
[9]Gal 5:24.
[10]Gal 2:20.
[11]Rom 4:25; Rom 6:6.
[12]Gregory IX, "*Mira circa nos*" in *Bullarium Franciscanum*, Giacinto Sbaraglia, ed., vol. 1 (Rome, 1759), 43; *FAED* 1, 567.
[13]This holocaust of "his own flesh" sounds like an expiation: "As it previously deceived him. . . . " For Gregory IX, here in perfect agreement with 1C 1-3, Francis was a former sinner, repentant, then converted to an exemplary, evangelical life. The link between stigmata and mortification is still suggested in L3C 14, but not in 2C 10-11 although this former legend here depends upon the previous one. See also AC 77.
[14]1C 90.

just as he has seen them a little while earlier on the crucified man hovering over him."[15]

Immediately after comes a very detailed description of Francis's hands, feet and right side. The hagiographer indicates that "only a few merited seeing the sacred wound in his side during his life." But Elias could see it, while Rufino "touched it." Indeed, Francis "hid those marks carefully from strangers, and concealed them cautiously from people close to him, so that even the brothers at his side and his most devoted followers for a long time did not know about them."[16] It was "his great secret."[17]

The third moment happens just after Francis's death. It was possible "to see in the middle of his hands and feet not just the holes of the nails, but the nails themselves formed by his own flesh, retaining the dark color of iron, and his right side red with blood." Not only the friars, but also the people, can kiss and see these five wounds.[18] When the body of Francis was brought to San Damiano, Clare and her sisters kissed them, too.[19]

We must remember that the legend of Thomas of Celano is not only a narration, but also the result of a judicial act, a real trial: the pontifical process of canonization. So Thomas needs to bring sure facts, certified by witnesses. I previously pointed out that each time he can indicate a witness for an episode, the hagiographer does it.[20] If we take the two passages describing the stigmata in the opposite order, it's obvious that Thomas has plenty of testimonies about Francis's wounds after his death, when his corpse was visible to everybody. For the period of Francis's life, Thomas doubtless knows several witnesses for the wounds of the hands and feet, but only two for the wound of the side. Two or three years after the funeral, in a legend written for the broadest circulation, it would have been absurd to give a false report about Francis's wounds, while a lot of people could have denounced the forgery.

---

[15] 1C 94.
[16] 1C 95.
[17] 1C 96.
[18] 1C 113.
[19] 1C 117.
[20] Dalarun, *The Misadventure*, 109-11.

So, my first conclusion, which is not based on personal faith but on the simple examination of the sources, is: In the moment of his death and in a previous period, Francis of Assisi bore wounds at his hands, his feet and his right side. I cannot call them "stigmata," because that would be a theological judgment. But I observe that the fifth wound is always placed by Thomas at Francis's right side. Thus, the physical conformity between Francis and the traditional representation of Christ is not an invention of Bonaventure or Giotto.

We saw that Thomas of Celano twice gives a precise description of the wounds, during the life of Francis and after his death. They are very clinical reports. It's obvious that the first one follows from the second one, given that the wounds could be examined at length only after Francis's death. In these descriptions, Thomas seems to borrow some words from the only author who spoke explicitly of the stigmata before him: Elias.[21] At the same time, his description is also in contradiction–a voluntary contradiction, I presume–with the previous description: "not just the holes of the nails, but the nails themselves formed by his own flesh."[22]

From Paul Sabatier on, many authors have presented Thomas as the servant of two authorities: Gregory IX and Elias.[23] But we can observe that, here, Thomas is not afraid to contradict both of them. In the *Mira circa nos*, the pope didn't describe wounds and didn't speak of "stigmata."[24] After Elias, Thomas chooses to use the word of Saint Paul[25] and mentions the five wounds with keen insistence. But while Elias described the stigmata as holes, Thomas replies: no, nails of flesh. I only see one reason to explain such an

---

[21] Here are the words that Thomas (mainly in 1C 89, 94-95, 98 and 112-113) could borrow from Elias's letter: *"gaudium," "miraculi novitatem," "non . . . auditum," "signum," "crucifixus," "stigmata Christi portans in corpore suo," "manus . . . et pedes," "clavorum," "parte confixas," "cicatrices," "latus," "lanceatum," "sanguinem."* The description by Thomas in 1C 112-13 of the "marvelous corpse" also comes from Elias.

[22] 1C 113.

[23] See Dalarun, *The Misadventure*, 127-31.

[24] It's a very expressive silence, given that, in the passage of the *Mira circa nos* I presume to be a reference to Francis's wounds, Gregory IX quotes Gal 5:24 and 2:20. Gal 5:24 is precisely quoted by Bonaventure in LMj 15:1 in relationship with the stigmata.

[25] Gal 6:17.

obstinacy: Thomas was sure his version was the truth. So I'm convinced that the description he gives is absolutely faithful.[26]

Elias was silent about the origin of the phenomenon. And Thomas is very embarrassed because he clearly knows nothing.[27] He has no witness and thus he must insist on Francis's absolute will of silence. He knows nobody who saw the original scene and Francis never spoke of it, since it was for him–Thomas says–a very private secret.[28] The hagiographer cannot indicate a sure date for the fact. His dating is only relative: two years before Francis's death. What does this mean? If Francis wanted to hide his wounds, it was only by chance some companions progressively saw them and they were unable to say exactly where Francis had been wounded. The only thing Thomas guesses is that there was perhaps a link between the mysterious event and a place: La Verna.[29] But his job is to tell. Thus he must tell something.

And so he did by trying to reconcile Elias and Gregory's presentations on this point. In the *Mira circa nos*, the pope mentions "the fire of love [*igne . . . charitatis*]." Thomas, who knows works of Gregory the Great and Bernard of Clairvaux on the topic,[30] remembers that the most beautiful symbol of burning love is the Seraph.[31] Re-

---

[26]Dalarun, *The Misadventure*, 129-30.

[27]When Miccoli comments, "Considerazioni," 27: "*Evidentemente della visione si sapeva ben poco e ben poco Francesco deve averne parlato,*" I totally agree, but in a more radical way, for I trust Thomas: obviously about the vision one knows nothing, and Francis must not have spoken of it at all.

[28]So the testimony of Roger of Wendover, who reports a long declaration of Francis about his wounds, must be rejected as very doubtful. The episode, the origin of which may be Elias's letter, was probably distorted by several oral reports; Schmucki, *The Stigmata*, 192-193; *FAED* 1, 600-601; Trexler, "The Stigmatized Body," 483-85 and 487-88.

[29]The reference to Gen 22:2 in the pope's letter ("the land of vision, on one of the mountains") may also have influenced the circumstances of the stigmatization in Thomas's tale. It is surely the choice of the place, La Verna, which leads to the dating, given that Thomas should have received testimonies about Francis's stay at La Verna in 1224.

[30]About the stigmata, Thomas of Celano follows exactly the works of Gregory the Great and Bernard of Clairvaux in 1C 113-114.

[31]See Schmucki, *The Stigmata*, 201-11. I think that the passage of Bernard of Clairvaux, "Sermones in Cantica canticorum," 19:5, in *Patrologia Latina*, vol. 183, 865, was the factor which triggered the presentation of Thomas. Indeed, in the same sentence, it includes the words *charitas* and *ignis*, like the *Mira circa nos*, and refers these elements

lying on Ezekiel and above all on Isaiah,[32] in a kind of typological exegesis between the old and the very new Franciscan testament, he tells the vision of the "man, having six wings like a Seraph." The wounds impressed in Francis's flesh are presented as the consequences of the impregnation of this novelty in his heart.[33]

I don't want to say that Thomas was a liar. He did his job like we do ours nowadays. But he knew—and we must know—that each time that he or his brothers spoke of the stigmata, each time that we, historians or theologians, speak about them we are in contradiction, according to Thomas himself, with Francis's clear and absolute will. This is a violation of a secret that he wanted to share only with God.[34]

If we must commit a violation, at least it was worthwhile stopping at Thomas's first report, because all the following ones add simple details or pure amplifications regarding his data.[35] Here again, we will start with the two descriptions of Francis's wounds, before studying the more delicate episode of La Verna.

---

to the Seraph. See also Hugo of Saint Victor, "Commentariorum in Hierarchiam coelestem S. Dionysii Areopagite secundum interpretationem Joannis Scoti . . . libri X" 6, in *Patrologia Latina*, vol. 175, 1031-44, where Hugo, who uses *seraphin*, *caritas* and *ignis*, often also uses also the word *holocauste* already present in his source, while *holocaustum* is present in Gregory's bull; I thank Dominique Poirel who has indicated to me this former reference.

[32]Isa 6:1-7. I summarize which seems to me the most simple textual way to explain the mental process which permits Thomas to build his narration of the stigmatization: from Elias' letter, he keeps mainly *miraculum, novitas, crucifixus* and *stigmata*; from Gregory's bull *visio, mons, ignis, charitas* and *crucifixus*; *charitas* and *ignis* stimulate in Thomas's mind the text of Bernard which offers him *seraphin*, a term which stirs up the verses of Isaiah. But more probably, like the reference to Hugo of Saint Victor quoted in the previous note suggests, Thomas has in mind not only one source, but a nebula of texts that he uses brilliantly to compose what I will call his "allegorical narration" or "narrative allegory." See the other possible, rich textual links suggested by Michael Cusato, "Of Snakes and Angels: The Mystical Experience Behind the Stigmatization Narrative of 1 Celano," pages 29-74, below.

[33]The best exegete of Thomas's tale is Bonaventure himself in the *Itinerarium Mentis in Deum* and in his sermons; FAED 2, 514-15, 722, 726-27, 734-35, 738-39, 742-43 and 757-58.

[34]On the significance of these wounds in Francis's spirit, see Miccoli, "Considerazioni," 35-39. I believe that Francis's wounds are in close relationship with the theological and moral thoughts he expresses in Adm 5-6.

[35]Perhaps the report of Roger of Wendover (see above, n. 28) and the passage of Jacques of Vitry's sermon which mentions "the traces of the wounds of Christ" on

Octavian Schmucki quite rightly noted a textual coincidence: In all the legends written after Celano's first *Life*, and not only these which come from the Franciscan Order,[36] the descriptions of the stigmata during Francis's life or after his death are exactly the same as in Thomas' report.[37] The first hagiographer puts special emphasis on this passage in his *Treatise of the Miracles*.[38] The only exceptions to the rule are the *Anonymous of Perugia* and the *Assisi Compilation*.[39] It's more than a textual borrowing–a very frequent phenomenon in the Franciscan hagiography; it's almost a quotation. The first clinical description of Thomas has become *the* canonical report of the fact. The clearest piece of evidence is the act, preserved in the communal archives of Assisi and probably drawn up in 1237, which gives a list of witnesses of Francis's wounds: the description they confirm is a simple quotation of the first *Life*.[40] In Alexander IV's bull, sent on October 29, 1255, the description of the wounds is clearly inspired again by Celano's words.[41]

Francis's body "at his death" depend directly on Elias; Schmucki, *The Stigmata*, 194-95; *FAED* 1, 589. For Schmucki, *The Stigmata*, 71-101, and Miccoli, "Considerazioni," 14-15, only those of Elias, Leo and Thomas are original testimonies. For me, the only three original testimonies are these of Elias, Gregory IX and Thomas. I agree with the position of Miccoli, "Considerazioni" 16, about the iconographic representations: "there is nothing new, nothing original, about this phenomenon." *[non ci dicono nulla di nuovo, di originario, sul fenomeno stesso.]*"

[36]VL XII, 55-61, and XIV, 15-20. Luke of Túy depends on 1C; Schmucki, *The Stigmata*, 278-79; *FAED* 1, 596. Bartholomew of Trent in his *Liber epilogorum in gesta sanctorum* depends on 1C; *FAED* 2, 784. James of Voragine in the *Golden Legend* depends on LCh and 3C; *FAED* 2, 796-97. Philippe Mousket depends on 1C; *FAED* 2, 806; Eudes of Châteauroux depends on 1C; *FAED* 2, 816. See also *Analecta Franciscana* 10 [Quaracchi, 1926-1941], 529-54 and 679-719, in particular 534-35, 536, 537, 539-40, 542, 543-44, 546-47, 686, 715-16 and 718.

[37]Schmucki, *The Stigmata*, 312-13; Miccoli, "Considerazioni," 24: "*Si configura quasi come una sorta di processo verbale.*" See LCh 11 and 13; Off 21 and 26/III-IV; LJS 62 (with some words probably reflecting Elias's Letter) and 71; L3C 69-70; 2C 135.

[38]3C 2 and 4-5.

[39]In AP 46, there is no real description of the wounds. In AC 94, the scars are evoked, but without description. In AC 118, there is a mention of the Seraph, but no mention of the stigmata.

[40]Michael Bihl, "De quodam elencho Assisiano testium oculatorum S. Francisci stigmatum," *Archivum Franciscanum Historicum* 19 (1926): 931-36; *FAED* 2, 770-71.

[41]Alexander IV, "*Benigna operatio,*" *Bullarium Franciscanum*, vol. 2 (Rome, 1761), 85-87; Schmucki, *The Stigmata*, 275-76; *FAED* 2, 779-81. LMj 13:3 and 15/2, and LMn 6:3, are inspired not only by Thomas's writings, but also by the bull of Alexander IV.

In regard to testimony concerning the presence of the wounds during Francis's life, among the hagiographers no one is able to add any new witnesses by name to the few companions Thomas first named,[42] except Thomas himself, who cites Brother Pacifico in his second legend[43] and Bonaventure, who evokes Alexander IV.[44] Usually, the only quoted names are still Elias and Rufino;[45] the omission of Elias is linked to the internal history of the Order, not to the stigmata themselves.[46] Only the act of 1237 brings new details, giving the names of four laypeople and one canon.[47]

Many brothers and the people of Assisi are cited as witnesses of the stigmata after Francis's death, while Clare and her sisters are sometimes forgotten.[48] The Act of 1237 gives the name of fourteen lay witnesses,[49] among which Jerome, who appears again in the *Major Legend* of Bonaventure.[50] In the *Treatise of the Miracles*, Thomas can add to the list "Brother Jacoba" of Settesoli[51] and he claims:

---

[42]L3C 69; 2C 135-36 and 138; LMn 6:3-5 and 9; "Legenda Monacensis 80-82," *Analecta Franciscana* 10 [Quaracchi, 1926-1941], 716-17. In this former legend, the witnesses remain very few, and emphasis is put on Francis's demand for secrecy, while, in UChL 2 for example, the tendency is that the few companions become many.

[43]2C 137.

[44]LMj 13:8. Actually, the words of the bull of Alexander IV sent on July 28, 1259, which are partially borrowed from the *Mira circa nos* of Gregory IX, don't really prove he was a personal eyewitness of the stigmata. Alexander IV, "Quia longum," *Bullarium Franciscanum*, vol. 2, 358-60; Schmucki, *The Stigmata*, 276: "When we held lesser positions . . . by a gift of God we merited at that time to have an intimate knowledge of this confessor."

[45]LJS 63; UChL 2; 2C 138, where Elias and Rufino are present, but anonymous, and 2C 214 where Francis hides his side; LMj 13:4-5 and 13:8-9, where Elias and Rufino are present, but anonymous.

[46]3C 4.

[47]*FAED* 2, 770-71. Arnaldo Fortini could easily identify them in the archives of the city.

[48]LCh 13: only the friars; LJS 71-72: the friars, Clare and her sisters; VL XIV:13-15, the presents; UChL 7-8: friars, people, Clare and her sisters; L3C 69-70: friars and people; "Legenda Monacensis 93," *Analecta Franciscana* 10 [Quaracchi, 1926-1941], 718, with friars and people.

[49]*FAED* 2, 770-71. Two more names are written after the description of the stigmata. They may be the names of the notaries who drew the act.

[50]LMj 15:4. In LMj 15:4-5, Bonaventure mentions the people, the brothers, Clare and her sisters.

[51]3C 39.

We who say these things have seen these things; we have touched with our hands what we are writing by hand. With tears in our eyes, we have sketched what we profess with our lips, and what we once swore, while touching sacred things, we declare for all time. Many brothers besides us saw it while the saint was alive; at his death, more than fifty of them with countless lay people venerated it.[52]

When did the Friars swear about the authenticity of the stigmata? Surely during the process of canonization in 1228. Indeed, the fact is belatedly confirmed by Gregory IX's letter sent on April 5, 1237. He wants to announce "a grand and unique miracle"–during Francis's life and after his death, he "was marked by God in his hands, feet and side with the likeness of the stigmata. When this was brought to our notice and to that of our brothers [cardinals] and was solemnly proved together with other miracles by witnesses most worthy of credibility, we had special reason for believing that . . . this same confessor should be added in the catalogue of the saints."[53] Gregory asks all the Christian people to trust this fact like he trusts himself and not to believe those who say the opposite.[54] Thanks to the marvelous article of André Vauchez, we know that this letter was among the first in a long collection of papal bulls on the same topic, always more detailed and vehement against the incredulous and detractors.[55] From the *Legend of the Three Compan-*

---

[52] 3C 5.

[53] These last words are partially borrowed from the *Mira circa nos*.

[54] Gregory IX, "Confessor Domini," *Bullarium Franciscanum* I, 214; Schmucki, *The Stigmata*, 273-74. The Life of Pope Gregory IX depends on 1C and the bull *Confessor Domini*; see *FAED* 1, 603-604.

[55] André Vauchez, "Les stigmates de saint François et leurs détracteurs dans les derniers siècles du Moyen Âge," *Mélanges d'archéologie et d'histoire* 80 (1968): 596-625; trans. as "The Stigmata of St. Francis and Its Medieval Detractors," *Greyfriars Review* 13 (1999): 61-89. See, in particular, 66: "Between 1237 and 1291 there were no fewer than nine papal bulls–some of which, it is true, merely repeated the earlier ones–denouncing those who denied the stigmata of St. Francis and severely condemning them." The first bull of Gregory IX about this issue, sent on March 31, 1237, was the *"Non minus dolentes."* See *Bullarium Franciscanum* I, 213. See also Saturnino Mencherini, *Codice diplomatico della Verna e delle SS. stimmate di S. Francesco d'Assisi nel VII° centenario del gran prodigio* (Florence: Tipografia Gualandi, 1924).

ions, the hagiographers mention the presence of detractors too and recount their miraculous punishment.[56]

André Vauchez perfectly explained the reasons of this opposition to or doubt about the stigmata, which were also present among the Friars.[57] But wasn't the first incredulous person Gregory IX, who never pronounced the word "stigmata" from 1228 to 1237? Why? Bonaventure is not afraid to recall the pope's reluctance and he explains it saying that, before the canonization, Gregory was not sure about the wound in the side.[58] As always, Bonaventure pretends to confront a problem in order to better avoid it. If Gregory received all the testimonies about Francis's wounds in 1228, he was perfectly aware that the corpse bore a wound on his right side too. And nevertheless, his doubt continued after the canonization. Thus, the pope's reluctance was not about the fact, since, according to my hypothesis, he discreetly mentioned it in the *Mira circa nos*, but about its cause. The other word he has hesitated to pronounce for nine years was the word "miracle."[59]

Vauchez notes that we have many references to the detractors, that we can understand their strategic reasons, but that the sources

---

[56]L3C 70; 3C 5-13; LMj 15:4; LMj Miracles 2-6; "Legenda Monacensis 80," *Analecta Franciscana* [Quaracchi, 1926-1941], 715.

[57]3C 10; see Dalarun, *The Misadventure*, 164-69. Between 1249 and 1254, John of Parma must order Brother Bonitius "to tell the brothers the truth about [Francis's] stigmata, because many in the world were doubting this matter;" *Tractatus fr. Thomae vulgo dicti de Eccleston de adventu fratrum minorum in Angliam*, ed. Andrew G. Little (Paris: Librarie Fischbacher, 1909), 93.

[58]LMj Miracles 2.

[59]Another question is: Why did he change his mind in 1237? Did he want to support Elias, who was the first to announce the stigmata, and who began to be attacked inside the Order at that moment? Did he want to support the Order in front of the whole Church? The simultaneity between the *Confessor Domini* (April 5, 1237) and the *Quoniam abundavit* (April 6, 1237) is a sign in favor of the second way. See Gregory IX, "*Quoniam abundavit*" in *Bullarium Franciscanum* I, 214-15; *FAED* 1, 576-77. But we cannot exclude a very sincere, spiritual meditation of the pope, which progressively would have pushed him to change his mind. According to Salimbene, *Cronica*, Giuseppe Scalia, ed., vol. 2 (Turnhout: Brepols, 1999), 579-80, in Off 26/III an antiphon for the Commemoration of Saint Francis is attributed to Gregory IX: "Lament, poor little company; to the father of the poor, like orphans cry: This sorrowful and plaintive sigh, Father Francis, take up and hear, and show to Christ those precious stigmata upon your side, and feet, and hands, that to us orphans He may give a worthy father in your stead."

are very discrete about the exact matter of the doubts. By antiphrasis, we can guess at least two of them. In the bull he sent on October 29, 1255, Alexander IV claims with insistence that the stigmata were impressed by "the hand of divine operation" and that the wound of the side "was not inflicted or made by man" [*humanitus*].[60] In the *Legenda Monacensis*, the hagiographer affirms that "this was not, like some envious slander, the result of the corruption of the scab."[61] We are not the only ones who have the formidable privilege of rationalism: Already in the middle of the thirteenth century, some people explained the stigmata by referring to a human cause (wounds voluntarily provoked) or a physiological cause (cutaneous infection). One century later, Petrarch defended the thesis that the wounds were due to what we would call today a psychosomatic origin.[62]

Once again, it means that the most mysterious problem remains the event of the stigmatization. I will not analyze the different narrations, since I strongly agree with Giovanni Miccoli that they are simple variations on Thomas's first composition. Chiara Frugoni commented on all of them. They can teach something about the reception of the phenomenon mainly in the Order, but nothing about the phenomenon itself. In a very positive way, I will try to respond

---

[60] Alexander IV, "*Benigna operatio*"; see *Bullarium Franciscanum* II, 85-87; Schmucki, *The Stigmata*, 275-76; *FAED* 2, 779-81.

[61] "Legenda Monacensis 80," *Analecta Franciscana* 10 [Quaracchi, 1926-1941], 715.

[62] Letter to Thomas of Garbo written on November 9, 1366; mentioned by Vauchez, "The Stigmata," 88, n. 85 and quoted by Giles Constable, *Three Studies in Medieval Religious and Social Thought* (Cambridge: Cambridge University Press, 1995), 219: "Surely the stigmata of Francis had their origin in the fact that he embraced the death of Christ in so constant and powerful a meditation that, when in his mind he had for a long time transferred it on to himself and seemed to himself attached to the cross with his Lord, at last his pious thought (*opinio*) transferred the true image of the thing from his mind onto his body." On a similar proposition of Peter Thomas (c. 1350), see Schmucki, *The Stigmata*, 37. But after all, these interpretations are not so far from Thomas's explanation in 1C 94: "While he was unable to perceive anything clearly understandable from the vision, its newness very much pressed upon his heart. Signs of the nails began to appear on his hands and feet, just as he has seen them a little while earlier on the crucified man hovering over him." And they are closer to the report found in L3C 14: "From that hour, therefore, his heart was wounded and it melted when remembering the Lord's passion. While he lived, he always carried the wounds of the Lord Jesus in his heart. This was brilliantly shown afterwards in the renewal of those wounds that were miraculously impressed on and most clearly revealed in his body."

to only two questions. Thomas of Celano fixed the place. What about the precise date and the witnesses?

Usually, it is admitted that the stigmatization happened on September 14, 1224. Actually, the first mention of such a dating appears only in 1246 in the *Legend of the Three Companions*, twenty-two years after the related fact, eighteen years after Thomas's report: "one morning, around the feast of the Exaltation of the Holy Cross."[63] If one of the companions would have known the exact date, he would have said it during the process and Thomas would have been able to date the mysterious event in his first *Life*.[64] But, already more precise than Elias ("not long before his death"), Thomas only said: "two years prior" to his death. As Francis died on October 4, 1226, it was easy to place the event of La Verna in 1224, close to the beginning of fall. The tale of Thomas was in obvious relationship with the crucifixion. And there is a famous feast which exalts the Holy Cross in the middle of September. So the author of the so-called *Legend of the Three Companions*[65] doesn't add anything to the first narration, if not an imprecise liturgical coincidence.[66]

Another of the three companions, Leo, also draws on his memories. Following Raoul Manselli,[67] I presume we find a trace of them in the *Assisi Compilation* and the Manuscript Little. In the *Assisi Compilation*, counting like his companions and perhaps relying on his own memory, he can fix the stay at La Verna around the feast of Saint Michael (September 29) and place it in the framework of a Lent invented by Francis, from the Assumption to the feast of the archangel.[68] This angelic figure stands in very convenient relation-

---

[63]L3C 69.

[64]See Schmucki, *The Stigmata*, 180: "Since the authority of later writers conveys no certainty, we must admit that we do not know the date on which St. Francis received the stigmata."

[65]Probably Brother Rufino of Assisi; see Jacques Dalarun and Jean-François Godet-Calogeras, "The Legend of the Three Companions: *Status Quaestionis* and New Perspectives," on the website of the Franciscan Institute http://www.sbu.edu.

[66]"Around [*circa*] the feast," the hagiographer says. This imprecision is a classic way to indicate more a spiritual relationship than a sure dating.

[67]Raoul Manselli, "Un giorno sulla Verna: San Francesco e frate Leone," *Frate Francesco* 50 (1983): 161-71, reprinted in Raoul Manselli, *Francesco e i suoi compagni* (Rome: Istituto Storico dei Cappuccini, 1995), 303-13.

[68]We have no remnant of this Lent in Francis's rules.

ship with the Seraph of Thomas. The miracle that the *Assisi Compilation* tells is not the stigmatization, but the songs of the birds. Yet the compiler adds:

> Among all the consolations, hidden and manifest, which the Lord granted him, there was shown to him by the Lord a vision of a Seraph, from which, for the whole time of his life, he had great consolation in his soul between himself and the Lord. And it happened that while his companion brought him food that day, he told him everything that happened to him.[69]

The actual novelty in Leo's memories is the story of the birds. He links it to the Seraph whom he probably knows at present through Thomas's first legend. Nothing allows us to think that Francis's confidences were precisely about the Seraph.[70] It would be hardly believable, since we learned from Thomas that the saint absolutely didn't want to speak about this.

Nevertheless, in the rubric he drew on the back of the *chartula* of the *Praises of God*, Leo gives the same dating for two events he links: on one hand the vision of the Seraph, his allocution and the impression of the stigmata, and on the other hand the composition of the *Praises* which happened during a Lent from the Assumption to the Saint Michael's feast.[71]

The special Lent of Francis in honor of Saint Michael returns in the *Remembrance of the Desire of a Soul* compiled by Thomas of Celano, but without any mention of the stigmata.[72] Quite to the contrary, when Thomas mentions the stigmata in the same legend,

---

[69]AC 118.

[70]The mention of the Seraph sounds like a confidential comment. "Everything that happened to him" [*omnia que sibi acciderant*] may be mainly linked with the previous episode of the birds.

[71]Attilio Bartoli Langeli, *Gli autografi di frate Francesco e di frate Leone* (Turnhout: Brepols, 2000), 31-32; Schmucki, *The Stigmata*, 181. See Enrico Menestò, "Introduzione," in *Il fatto delle stimmate*, 9-12.

[72]2C 197.

[73]2C 135-139.

he doesn't give any indication of date, but hammers again at Francis's will to absolutely hide the wounds.[73] In the *Umbrian Choir Legend*[74] or in the *Treatise of the Miracles*,[75] the hagiographer still retains the dating for the stigmatization given in the first *Life*: two years before the saint's death. The synthesis of all the chronological elements is done by Bonaventure: the stay at La Verna is a Lent in honor of Saint Michael[76] and the stigmatization happens on the feast of the Exaltation of the Holy Cross.[77] I don't believe these dates have a real historical value. They sound like the product of a textual, progressive construction.

And so there remains only one problem: was Leo present or not during the stigmatization? We already observed that, in the *Assisi Compilation*, the anonymous companion who stays with Francis at La Verna doesn't see the scene of the Seraph. Even the songs of the birds and the attacks of the devils are only told to him by Francis.[78] In the Manuscript Little, still at La Verna but without dating, when an anonymous companion receives the *Praises of God* and a benediction written by Francis, the stigmata are not mentioned.[79]

In the *Remembrance* of Thomas, the same episode is present, still with an anonymous companion and without any link with the stigmata.[80] If Leo would have got some precious information about the stigmatization, why wouldn't he have given them to Thomas at least in 1246? Thus, his famous autograph on the back of the *Praises of*

---

[74]UChL 1; *Analecta Franciscana* 10 [Quaracchi, 1926-1941], 543-54.
[75]3C 5.
[76]LMj 13:1.
[77]LMj 13:3. Both dates are expressed in LMn 6:1.
[78]AC 118.
[79]*Un nouveau manuscrit franciscain ancien Phillipps 12290 aujourd'hui dans la bibliothèque de A. G. Little*, A.G. Little, ed. (Paris: Librarie Fischbacher, 1914-1919), #154, 70.
[80]2C 49. The same episode is present in LMj 11:9 and LMn 4:6: The companion is still unnamed. He is finally called Leo only in the *Considerazion sulle stimmate* 2. In *Considerazioni* 3, there is still no witness for the apparition of the Seraph and the stigmatization. Leo becomes here the brother who could touch the wounds instead of Rufino: it's a mere substitution; *I Fioretti di san Francesco: Considerazioni sulle stimmate Vita di frate Ginepro Vita del beato Egidio Cantico di frate Sole e dell'altre creature*, Eliodoro Mariani, ed. (Vicenza: Lief, 1977).

God must be posterior to this date. Leo, involved in his continuous remembering of the Franciscan past, connects in his rubric the two episodes of La Verna he separately mentioned in 1246–Seraph and *Praises*—[81]and links them with the stigmatization told by Thomas. According to the testimony of Thomas of Eccleston, Leo, without explicitly connecting the Seraph with the stigmatization, would have claimed that the apparition happened "much more clearly than is described in his Life."[82]

Let's summarize what we can guess about Leo's testimony. Certainly, he was at La Verna between summer and fall 1224, and there he received, written by Francis's hand, the *Praises of God* and his benediction. He likely took advantage of Francis's intimate recollections about the special Lent he wanted to respect, and about some visions like the songs of the birds or the attacks of the devils. But Leo didn't realize that Francis began to bear the five wounds from that moment. Anyhow, he is never cited by the hagiographers as a witness of the stigmata[83] or of the stigmatization. Reading the first *Life* of Thomas after the saint's death, he understood that he missed a prodigious event. So he started to mentally connect La Verna, the Lent of Saint Michael and, very discreetly, the vision of the Seraph

---

[81]Bartoli Langeli, *Gli autografi*, 31-32: "Beatus Franciscus duobus annis ante mortem suam **fecit quadragesimam** in loco **Alverne ad honorem beate Virginis matris dei et beati Michaelis** archangeli a festo Assumptionis sancte Marie Virginis usque ad festum sancti Michaelis septembris. **et facta est** super eum manus **domini** [Ez. 1, 3] post **visionem** et allocutionem **seraphym** et impressionem stigmatum christi in corpore suo: fecit has laudes ex alio latere cartule scriptas. et manu sua scripsit gratias agens deo de beneficio sibi collato. Beatus franciscus scripsit manu sua istam benedictionem mihi fratri leoni." In bold are the parallels with AC 118; in underlining with Little 154.

[82]*Tractatus fr. Thomae*, 93; Schmucki, "The Stigmata," 186-87. In this passage, Rufino likely mentions implicitly the stigmatization when he says that "the angel treated . . . harshly" Francis. See Miccoli, "Considerazioni," 30-31; and ibid., 31-32 about the Life of Giles.

[83]See above n. 80. The testimony of Salimbene according to which Leo would have described Francis "like one crucified deposed from the Cross" is probably authentic (Salimbene actually knew that Leo really said that), but Leo's description is a borrowing from 1C 112; Salimbene, *Cronica*, vol. 1, Giuseppe Scalia, ed. (Turnhout: Brepols, 1998), 296. See Miccoli, "Considerazioni," 32-33.

in the records he compiled in 1246; then La Verna, the Lent, the Seraph, the stigmata and the *Praises* in the rubric of the *chartula*.[84]

It's time to conclude. At an uncertain date before his death, in an uncertain place, Francis began to have five wounds similar to the traditional representation of Christ's traces of crucifixion,[85] which few companions saw, but that everybody could contemplate after his death. We cannot know the origin of these wounds, given that all the reports we have preserved about the event are mere speculations of the brothers and, first of all, of Thomas of Celano. Deprived of any testimony on the fact, the first hagiographer only could write a kind of narrative allegory, which was then understood by everyone as a historical narration. On this point at least, we are obliged to respect the secret of Francis.

But we can say, mainly thanks to Giles Constable,[86] that there is a point which all the brothers after Elias, the popes and many historians up to today have mistakenly claimed, that is, that the stigmata of Francis were an absolute novelty.[87] In the *Life of Dominic Loricatus*

---

[84]This rubric was probably written even after LMj; Trexler, "The Stigmatized Body," 464, n. 7. Miccoli, "Considerazioni," 28, believes that the rubric is older; nevertheless, he considers the reference to the Seraph's allocution as a sign of a late redaction.

[85]I agree with Miccoli in believing that, later on, the iconography cannot reveal any real information about the phenomenon of the stigmatization (see above, n. 35), but I surmise, with Constable, *Three Studies*, 162-63, 180-82, 199 and 221-23, that, before, it played a very important role in the mind of the stigmatics.

[86]Giles Constable, "The Ideal of the Imitation of Christ," in *Three Studies*, 143-248, especially 194-217, "The Imitation of the Body of Christ."

[87]Constable, *Three Studies*, 215: "Francis of Assisi is often said to have been the first stigmatic, and he is probably the first person to have had visible marks which are known from precise early descriptions to have resembled those of Christ and which are not known to have been imposed on his body by himself or others, but he was not the first person to have borne marks of suffering which were considered to resemble the wounds of Christ." Also, at page 217: "These cases show that Francis of Assisi was not an isolated example of an otherwise unknown and unprecedented phenomenon but the best-authenticated and most influential case of a physical condition which had a long background in the religious history of the eleventh and twelfth centuries and of which there were other examples, varying in character and affecting different types of people, male and female as well as lay, clerical, and monastic. The stigmata of Francis were exceptional, however, because from the moment of their discovery they were believed to be of supernatural origin and to show the perfection of his imitation of Christ and his apocalyptic role as a second Christ."

written in the eleventh century by Peter Damian, one can read this passage: "Our Dominic bore the stigmata of Jesus in his body and not only had he painted the banner of the Cross on his front, but he had also impressed it on all sides in all his members."[88] The hagiographer was neither a liar nor a heretic. He was cardinal of the Roman Church. And Dominic was not a swindler. Like Francis, he was a fool for Christ.

---

[88]Peter Damian, "Vita sancti Rodulphi episcopi Eugubini et s. Dominici Loricati" in *Patrologia Latina*, vol. 144, 1024. When I discussed Chiara Frugoni's book, I already quoted this passage in Jacques Dalarun, *Francesco: un passaggio: Donna e donne negli scritti e nelle leggende di Francesco d'Assisi* (Rome: Viella, 1994), 17, n. 15. See also the English translation: *Francis and the Feminine* (St. Bonaventure, NY: Franciscan Institute Publications, 2006). Constable, *Three Studies*, 202-203, comments: "This is the first known reference to what may have been the reproduction of Christ's stigmata on a living person, but it is hard to tell how explicitly Damiani's words should be taken, especially in view of his biblical terminology." The passage is at length analyzed by Trexler in "The Stigmatized Body," 474-76. Dominic died on October 14, 1060, in the hermitage of Frontale. Fonte Avellana, Camaldoli and La Verna are very close to each other.

OF SNAKES AND ANGELS:
THE MYSTICAL EXPERIENCE BEHIND THE
STIGMATIZATION NARRATIVE
OF 1 CELANO

MICHAEL F. CUSATO

Part I: The Account of the Stigmatization of Francis

Images, visual depictions and iconographical representations are compelling means of conveying to the human observer the content of historical events, written narratives and ideas. Such depictions arrest the attention, stir the emotions and impress upon the imagination lasting memories of what has been observed or contemplated in ways that other, more discursive forms of learning often do not. If it is true that the so-called Millennial Generation, born and raised in the age of videos and DVDs, has a learning-style that is decisively prejudiced in favor of the visual, it must also be said that human beings in every generation have often learned and assimilated such content most personally through the medium of images.[1]

Though separated by a millennium of years, men and women in the High Middle Ages were no exception to this general observation. Indeed, the use of sculpted capitals in cathedrals and monastic churches, of painted and carved crucifixes, of statuary of the Madonna and Child and of the saints, as well as the innovation of the technique of stained-glass (the famous *biblia pauperum*): all testify to the reality that people often learn (and perhaps learn more effectively) through the medium of artistic representations which translate story, event and idea into image.

---

[1] On the learning styles of the so-called "Millennials," see, for example: Diane Olinger, "Boomers, Gen-Xers and Millennials: Understanding the New Students," *Educause Review* 38.4 (2003): 37-47; and Lynna J. Ausburn and Floyd B. Ausburn, "Desktop Virtual Reality: A Powerful New Technology for Teaching and Research in Industrial Teacher Education," *Journal of Industrial Teacher Education* 41.4 (Winter, 2004) = http://scholar.lib.vt.edu/ejournals/JITE/v41n4/.

When it comes to the Franciscan story, the single event in the life of Francis that has received the most attention by artists and iconographers in the Middle Ages and Renaissance must surely be the stigmatization of St. Francis. From the early depiction of the event by Bonaventura Berlinghieri of Lucca to the famous fresco by Giotto in the Basilica of San Francesco in Assisi to the magnificent renaissance tableau by Domenico Ghirlandaio, centuries of men and women have become familiar with the mystery of Francis's stigmatization by meditating upon and praying through the varied representations of that event in which, according to the early Franciscan sources, Francis is said to have received the wound-marks of Jesus's passion in the autumn of 1224 while on the mountain of La Verna.

And yet, images–be they painted, carved, sculpted or fired into glass–are the end-result of a complex and subtle interaction between the imagination of their authors and the sources upon which they are ostensibly based. In the case of the stigmatization of Francis, leaving aside the announcement by Brother Elias of Cortona in his encyclical letter upon the death of Francis of this *novitas miraculi* of the stigmata,[2] it is Thomas of Celano, the papally-commissioned hagiographer of the Franciscan Order, who was the first person to attempt to put into **narrative** form an experience which neither he nor probably any other friar witnessed themselves.[3] Celano's account will then be taken up later and expanded upon, for example, by the author who wrote the so-called *Legend of the Three Companions*, Bonaventure in his *Legenda maior* and, considerably later, the author of the *Actus beati Francisci et*

---

[2]*Epistola encyclica de transitu S. Francisci a fr. Helia tunc ordinis vicario generali ad omnes provincias Ordinis missa*, 523-28 in *Analecta Franciscana* X, esp. 526. The same phrase will be taken up Thomas of Celano and used by him in the *Vita prima* (1 Cel 112).

[3]Thomas of Celano, *Vita prima S. Francisci*, 94-96 in *Analecta Franciscana* X, pp. 72-74. Julian of Speyer (*Vita S. Francisci*, chaps. 61-63 in *Analecta Franciscana* X, 363-64) and Henri d'Avranches (*Legenda versificata*, XII, lines 35-69 in *Analecta Franciscana*, X, 478-79) merely adapted Celano's account to their own commissioned purposes. Nor should one forget the allusion to the wounds of the poor Christ on the cross and the sealing (with his wounds) of those who would follow him in poverty found in the *Sacrum commercium* (written perhaps between 1237-38); cf. *Sacrum commercium beati Francisci cum Domina paupertate*, ch. 6, ed. Stefano Brufani (S. Maria degli Angeli: Edizioni Porziuncola, 1990), 142 [= Quaracchi edition, ch. 21].

socii eius (a Latin version of the later Italian text known as the *Fioretti*).[4] These are the narrative accounts, which when filtered through the imagination of the artist, have given us the visual representations that have formed in our own minds what this event might have looked like and meant.

What I would like to demonstrate in these pages is my contention that the iconographical representations, while certainly compelling and illuminating, can also at the same time be open to misreading and misinterpretation—and this on two levels. First, what do we, as audience or observer of a work of art, bring to our visual experience? What presuppositions or assumptions about the event do we read into an artist's representation? And second, it must be said that, ultimately, the end-product of an artist's artistry is largely dependent upon that artist's own understanding of the sources, anecdotes and testimonies of others from which he or she is drawing inspiration. This observation then leads us to ask two further questions. First: how did a given artist—a Giotto, for example—read or understand the literary accounts of the stigmatization found in Celano and Bonaventure, and then render that understanding into visual imagery? And second: how did Celano and Bonaventure themselves read and understand the event of the stigmatization of Francis? It is the second question only—the literary rather than the artistic representation—that I am proposing to explore in this essay. And I will do so primarily through a study of the first narrative account given to us by Thomas of Celano.

But before I enter into an examination of the texts themselves, let me begin by making a few brief comments about the sources. First, the primary accounts of this great event in the life of Francis (one can even say in the life of the Franciscan Order—so important will it be for minorite self-understanding in the 1230s and 1240s)[5]—are essentially

---

[4] The texts of these accounts are cited below.

[5] Cf. Michael F. Cusato, *La renonciation au pouvoir chez les Frères Mineurs au 13e siècle*, Diss. PhD, Université de Paris IV–Sorbonne (1991), chapter 2: pp. 181-234; but esp. 218-28 (on the meaning of Francis laid out in the hymns of Gregory IX, spurred by a deepening reflection on the significance of his stigmata). An English translation of the dissertation is still in preparation.

five: (1) 1 Celano 91-96 (esp. 94-95);[6] (2) 3 Soc. 69-70;[7] (3) 3 Cel 2-13 (esp. 4-5);[8] (4) Bonaventure's *Legenda maior*, XIII, 1-9 (esp. 1-3);[9] and (5) the highly elaborated account found in the *Actus beati Francisci et sociorum eius*, IX (or its Italian version in the *Fioretti*).[10] Furthermore, I am going to focus almost exclusively on the account of the *Vita prima* of Thomas of Celano (which, being the first, is the foundational account) while adding a few details from other sources when they add something critical to the overall picture.[11] In doing so, I will be placing a certain amount of emphasis on the details provided in the account of the *Actus beati Francisci et sociorum eius* since, even though a very late source, it bears the traces of a long and cherished oral tradition among the friars who were present with him on La Verna.[12] For it ought to be kept in mind that Celano was not trying to narrate all the events that occurred there. We know from other sources, notably Leo, that there were indeed other events that did occur there.

---

[6]Thomas of Celano, *Vita prima s. Francisci*, 91-96, esp. pp. 94-95 in *Analecta Franciscana* X, 69-74, esp. pp. 72-73.

[7]See 3 Soc 69-70, in Théophile Desbonnets, "Legenda trium Sociorum. Édition critique," *AFH* 67 (1974): 38-144, esp. 142-43. There is only the briefest mention of the stigmatization–a mere line–in the earlier text upon which 3 Soc. is in part dependent, the *Anonymous of Perugia* (1240-41): cf. AP 46b, p. 102.

[8]Thomas of Celano, *Tractatus de miraculis b. Francisci*, *Analecta Franciscana* X, 2-13, pp. 272-78, esp. 4-5, pp. 273-74.

[9]Bonaventure, *Legenda maior*, *Analecta Franciscana* 10, XIII/1-9, pp. 615-20, esp. 1-3, pp. 615-17.Cf. also the *Legenda minor* VI in *Analecta Franciscana* X, 672-75.

[10]*Actus beati Francisci et sociorum eius*, IX/68-70, eds. Jacques Cambell, Marino Bigaroni and Giovanni Boccali (S. Maria degli Angeli: Edizioni Porziuncola, 1988), 172; cf. also the much expanded version of the events found in the "Third Consideration of the Stigmata" found, for example, in *I Fioretti di san Francesco*, ed. Arnaldo della Torre (Turin: G.B. Paravia, 1921), 220-32.

[11]For an even closer examination of the development of the description of the stigmata in many of these same narrative accounts as well as the papal comments on the matter, see the excellent article of Jacques Dalarun, "The Great Secret of Francis," also found in this volume. He is the first, it seems, to notice the allusions to the stigmata and the Seraph in *Mira circa nos*, the bull of canonization.

[12]This is admittedly a rather perilous hermeneutical strategy. One should not, however, dismiss out-of-hand the details provided by the fourteenth-century account. One cannot simply assume that every new detail that appears in a later narrative is willy-nilly a fanciful elaboration added for polemical purposes. The historical validity of new elements always needs to be tested against other evidence already accepted as credible.

Celano's intention was to describe with the language of his classical training and hagiographical art what he believed might have occurred during that mysterious event on that momentous day. Later on, friars associated with those who had been with him on La Verna will take it upon themselves–for their own reasons–to contextualize that momentous event with information about the broader experiences of those who had shared that time together.

If we take into account the principal narratives of the events that probably took place on La Verna, we can summarize–very briefly– what might have occurred in the following manner:

- First, at some time in late July or early August 1224, Francis decided to make a "Lent of St. Michael"–that is, a fast lasting roughly from August 15 (the day of the feast of the Assumption) to September 29 (the feast of St. Michael the Archangel) at a place given to the friars for their use as a hermitage by Count Orlando di Chiusi: La Verna.[13] He took with him several companions, including most notably Brothers Leo, Masseo, Angelo and Illuminato.[14]
- Second, at some point during this time, Bro. Leo apparently approached Francis with some kind of personal crisis which Francis helped to ease through the writing of a famous blessing for him contained on what is now called the *chartula* of St. Francis.[15] Although the *Considerazioni sulle stimmate* places this crisis **before** the stigmatization, there is, as we shall see, good reason to believe that it will actually have occurred **after** the event rather than before it.[16]

---

[13]The account of Francis's fast on La Verna with several of his companions in 1224 found in the *Actus* depicts the giving of this land to the friars within a relatively close time period to the stigmatization event by Count Orlando di Chiusi.

[14]The first three names are supplied by *Actus*, IX/23, p. 128. Bonaventure (LM IX/4) is the only source in the thirteenth century to attest to the presence of Illuminato on La Verna. The account in the *Fioretti* borrows its attestation from this latter source.

[15]I will discuss this importance of the *chartula* and its relationship to the event of the stigmata in the second half of the article.

[16]An account of a crisis supposedly experienced by Leo is found only in the "Second Consideration on the Stigmata," *I Fioretti* (pages 211-12). The account given in 2 Cel 49 seems to be a little closer to the actual chronology of events, although there is no

- Third, on or around the Feast of the Exaltation of the Cross,[17] Francis either picks up (or is given) a "volume where the Holy Gospels were written," opens it and begins meditating upon the passion of Christ.[18]

---

mention at all of the stigmatization which, by Leo's own testimony, is the cause of the writing of the *Praises of God*.

[17] The phrase–and the approximate dating of the event to this feast–occurs first in the *Legenda trium sociorum*, c. 69: *"quodam mane circa festum Exaltationis sanctae Crucis."* Bonaventure, following the lead of the author of 3 Soc, uses the exact same phrase both in the LMaj XIII/3 and LMin VI/1. Curiously, Celano does not explicitly reference the feast; nor does Leo in his annotations on the *chartula* (though added after the writing of 3 Soc). In the former case, Dalarun, in his aforementioned article in this volume, believes Celano's silence on this matter represents an important controlling datum, casting doubt upon the veracity of the association of the feast with the stigmatization. I am not entirely persuaded. Celano mentions neither the presence of Leo (or any other companions) nor even the writing of the *chartula*; and yet both issues are considered crucial for understanding the events that occurred on La Verna. Its absence in Celano is perhaps curious but not necessarily critical to his understanding of the event. The hagiographer does report an opening of the Gospels in the pericope that *precedes* the stigmatization account (see text in next note). What is crucial for Celano is not the feast day association but rather, as we will see, the text that Francis may have been meditating on. Interestingly, the *Instrumentum de stigmatibus beati Francisci*, a document incorporated into the *Chronica XXIV generalium* but reporting a testimony from 1281 (written in 1282), testifies that the event coincided *exactly* with the feast: *"In mane ergo diei Exaltationis sanctae Crucis summo diluculo exiens cellam in vehementissimo fervore spiritus ad locum quendam orationi solitum properabam"* (*Analecta Francescana* 3 [Quaracchi, 1897], 643). It seems that there was a debate of some importance at this time about the relationship of the stigmatization event to the feast of the Exaltation of the Cross.

[18] 1 Cel 92: "So one day he approached the sacred altar which had been built in the hermitage where he was staying and, taking up the volume where the Holy Gospels were written *(accepto codice, in qua sacra Evangelia errant conscripta)*, he placed it reverently upon the altar. Then he prostrated himself . . . asking . . . that God . . . be pleased to show him his will. He prayed earnestly that at the first opening of the book he would be shown what was best for him to do. . . .He took the book from the altar and opened it. . . ." Celano then goes on to write that, in the manner of other saints, he opened the book *(libri apertione)* three times and each time his eyes alighted on an account of the suffering and passion of Jesus Christ or texts alluding to such. Celano is obviously placing Francis's actions within the wider context of the prayer of other Christian saints. This will be key. Similarly but with slight differences, Bonaventure (LMaj XIII/2) has Francis take the book from the altar and had his companion (Leo) open it three times. The *Legend of the Three Companions*, predating Bonaventure, has no opening of any book, no altar and no companions being present. Critically, the formulations used in these sources make it difficult to determine precisely what it was that Francis actually opened. Was it a

- Fourth, during this period of profound prayer, he has what perhaps can best be described as a kind of mystical transport, depicted by Celano as a vision of a Seraph hovering above him and resulting in the appearance on his body of the wound-marks of the Crucified Jesus: the stigmata. The word is, of course, borrowed from Paul's *Letter to the Galatians* (6:17) in which he declares himself to be "bearing the brand-marks of Jesus in [his] own body."[19]
- Fifth, shortly after this vision, Francis asks for a piece of parchment (the aforementioned *chartula*) and writes the *Praises of God* on its front (or *recto*) side.
- And sixth, on the back (or *verso*) side he writes the famous prayer of Aaron from Numbers 6 and then traces the famous Tau emerging from the mouth of a mysterious head and the so-called *Blessing to Brother Leo*. Annotations in red ink, commenting on some of these same events, were added at a later time by Leo (who retained possession of the *chartula*).

Thus, to recap the essential moments of this event: the opening of a book containing texts from the gospels and a meditation on the passion of Christ on (or around) the Feast of the Exaltation of the Cross; the mystical vision of the Seraph and the appearance of the

---

Bible? Was it a missal containing the reading of the liturgy? Was it book containing the Gospels? Was it the Gospels from the liturgical year? Given the fact that Celano has this book located near an altar in the hermitage, it seems reasonable to conclude that the book was either a missal with the readings for the liturgy (including the liturgical feasts of the year) or possibly even the famous evangeliary which Francis had had compiled at some point for his meditation, containing the scriptural readings from the liturgical year and now found at the back of Francis's breviary. On this latter issue see: Laurent Gallant, "L'évangéliaire de saint François d'Assise," *Collectanea Francescana* 53 (1983): 5-22. Note, however, that at least in this collection, the text for the feast of the Exaltation of the Cross is John 12: 31-36 (p. 18, no. 221). The text of John 3:1-16 was used *"In inventione sancte crucis"* (p. 17, no. 205), traditionally celebrated on 3 May in the West (but 13 September in the East). Celano's description, however, would seem to be more in line with a missal/lectionary than the evangeliary.

[19]Gal 6: 17: *De cetero nemo mihi molestus sit: ego enim stigmata Domini Iesu in corpore meo porto*. All texts from Scripture cited in Latin are from the Vulgate.

stigmata in his body; the writing on the front side of the *chartula*; and finally, the writing on the back side of the same piece of parchment.

Now, my intention here is both stunningly simple and frightfully complex: namely, to understand, as best as we can, what might actually have happened during this mystical transport and how it came to be written up by Celano in the manner in which he did.

So let us begin with the text of 1 Celano 94:

> While he was staying in that hermitage called La Verna, after the place where it was located, two years prior to the time that he returned his soul to heaven, he saw *in the vision of God* a man, *having six wings like a Seraph, standing over* him, *arms extended and feet joined*, affixed to a cross. *Two of his wings* were raised up, *two were stretched out over his head as if for flight*, and *two covered his* whole *body*. When the blessed servant of the Most High saw these things, he was filled with the greatest awe, but could not decide what this vision meant for him. Moreover, he greatly rejoiced and was much delighted by the kind and gracious look that he saw the Seraph gave him. The Seraph's beauty was beyond comprehension, but the fact that the Seraph was fixed to the cross and the bitter suffering of that passion thoroughly frightened him. Consequently he got up both sad and happy as joy and sorrow took their turns in his heart. Concerned over the matter, he kept thinking about what this vision could mean and his *spirit was anxious* to discern a sensible meaning from the vision. While he was unable to perceive anything clearly under-standable from the vision, the strangeness of it very much perplexed his heart. Signs of the nails began to appear on his hands and feet, just as he had seen them a little while earlier on the crucified man hovering over him.[20]

---

[20]1 Cel 94: "*Faciente ipso moram in eremitorio, quod a loco in quo positum est Alverna nominatur, duobus annis antequam animam redderet caelo, vidit in visione Dei virum unum, quasi Seraphim sex alas habentem, stantem supra se, manibus extensis ac pedibus coniunctis,*

Celano's account pivots on the description of what Francis "saw" (or, to be more accurate, experienced) in this moment of intense prayer. One must keep in mind that Celano is trying to put language on someone else's spiritual, even mystical, experience, rendering what is essentially ineffable into understandable human terms and images. He then describes what Francis saw in this vision as "a man having six wings like a Seraph": two of his wings were above his head, two covered his feet and two covered his body. Then, as the vision disappeared, marks that apparently looked like nails began to appear on his hands, his feet and his right side. After the vision, however, Francis decided not only to hide these wounds as best as he could but also–or so we are told by later commentators like Bonaventure in the *Legenda maior* and Leo in his additions to the *chartula*–to remain silent on the content of a message[21] given to him in the experience.[22]

---

cruci affixum. Duae alae supra caput elevabantur, duae ad volandum extendebantur, duae denique totum velabant corpus. Cumque ista videret beatus servus Altissimi, admiratione permaxima replebatur, sed quid sibi vellet haec visio advertere nesciebat. Gaudebat quoque plurimum et vehementius laetabatur in benigno et gratioso respectu, quo a Seraphim conspici se videbat, cuius pulchritudo inaestimabilis erat nimis, sed omnino ipsum cruces affixio et passionis illius acerbitas deterrebat. Sicque surrexit, ut ita dicatur, tristis et laetus, et gaudium atque moeror suas in ipso alternabant vices. Cogitabat sollicitus, quid posset haec visio designare, et ad capiendum ex ea intelligentiae sensum anxiabatur plurimum spiritus eius. Cumque liquido ex ea intellectu aliquid non perciperet et multum eius cordi visionis huius novitas insideret, coeperunt in manibus eius et pedibus apparere signa clavorum, quemadmodum paulo ante virum supra se viderat crucifixum."

[21]The word Leo uses on the *chartula* is *"allocutio."*

[22]Celano (and those accounts dependent on his in the 1230s) attests to the silence of Francis on the matter of having received the marks of the stigmata, lest he lose the grace associated with so great a gift–a typical hagiographical motif. It is Bonaventure's account that adds to this assertion the following tantalizing detail: "Then, with much fear, he recounted the vision in detail, adding that the one who had appeared to him had *told him some things which he would never disclose to any person* as long as he lived. We should believe, then, that *those utterances (illa eloquia) of that sacred Seraph* marvelously appearing to him on the cross were so secret (*arcana*) that people are not permitted to speak of them" (LMaj XIII:4). It is quite possible that Bonaventure borrowed this detail from the testimony of Brother Leo which appears on the top of the verso side of the *chartula* where he refers to the *"visio et allocutio"* of the Seraph. In Bonaventure's account, it is Illuminato, another companion present on La Verna, who was trying to get Francis to share with others the mystery of the stigmata–a plea which prompted Francis to reveal

If we are to penetrate into the heart of this experience, it is incumbent upon us to read Thomas of Celano's text very closely–what it says and what it does not say. However, the key to knowing how to read Thomas' language–and especially the images he deliberately chose to use–is actually found elsewhere.[23] That key is found in recalling that this experience might have occurred, according to the author of the *Legend of the Three Companions*, "around the Feast of the Exaltation of the Cross."

The gospel that would have been read on that feast was either the text of John 12: 31-36 or John 3:1-16.[24] It is the latter text–the more evocative one–that is of interest to us here. The main part of this gospel reads as follows:

---

that there was also a "message" given in the experience as well. The transmission of such a message gets transformed into a "secret message" given in a "secret conversation" in the "Third Consideration of the Stigmata" in *I Fioretti* (cf. pages 228-31).

[23]In his above-mentioned article in this volume, Jacques Dalarun proposes a different but, in some respects, complementary explanation of the sources of Celano's account. When combined, the two approaches illustrate the profundity and sophistication of Celano's reflection upon the event.

[24]It is difficult for us to know with certitude the gospel text that Francis might have been meditating on that day (if the experience did indeed coincide with the feast itself). For not only do we not know with precision what kind of *"codex"* Francis might have had access to on La Verna (was it an evangeliary or a missal?); but, in the latter instance, we do not even know *which* missal (and lectionary) Francis might have had at his disposal. For whereas most lectionaries in use since the eighth century would have had John 3: 1-15 as the feast day gospel, there is real uncertainty as to whether the *codex* would have been this traditional lectionary (since increasingly outdated in Italy) or the newer Lateran missal being promoted by the Roman Curia especially since Honorius III (which changed the gospel reading to John 12: 31-36). This latter reading retains the motif of exaltation but in a rather different context: "Now has judgment come upon this world; now will this world's prince be driven out; and I–*once I am lifted up from the earth*–will draw all to myself. (This statement indicated the sort of death he had to die)" [vv. 31-33]. At this stage of my research, it is a question which admits of no definitive answer. On these thorny problems, see Louis van Tongeren, *Exaltation of the Cross: Toward the Origins of the Feast of the Cross and the Meaning of the Cross in Early Medieval Liturgy*, Liturgia Condenda, 11 (Leuven: Peeters, 2000), 62-66, 68-73; and 115-18. We will see, however, that the real issue is less which text might have been read by Francis and on which day as it is which text (and its associated imagery) **Celano** believed might have been formative in Francis's prayer on La Verna. And for him, that text would probably have been John 3:13-17.

[Jesus said to Nicodemus]:

¹³"No one has gone up to heaven except the One who came down from there–the Son of Man [who is in heaven]. ¹⁴For just as Moses lifted up the serpent in the desert, so must the Son of Man be lifted up, ¹⁵that all who believe may have eternal life in him. ¹⁶ For God so loved the world that he gave his only Son, that whoever believes in him may not die but may have eternal life.²⁵

For our purposes here (though the whole text would be important for understanding the totality of the experience of Francis), it is the earlier part of the text–the particular image used by the Evangelist–that concerns us, where verse 14 reads: ***"For just as Moses lifted up the serpent in the desert, so too must the Son of Man be lifted up."*** What is crucial to appreciate is that behind this vivid and striking image used by the Fourth Evangelist in the Gospel of John stands the Old Testament text of Numbers 21: 4-9 which describes the travails experienced by Moses in leading the Israelites out of Egypt through the wilderness of Sinai.²⁶ That account reads:

⁴From Mount Hor they set out on the Red Sea road to bypass the land of Edom. But with their patience worn out by the

---

²⁵John 3:13-17 in the Vulgate: "*Et nemo ascendit in caelum, nisi qui descendit de caelo, Filius hominis, qui est in caelo. Et sicut Moyses exaltavit serpentem in deserto, ita exaltari oportet Filium hominis: ut omnis qui credit in ipsum, non pereat, sed habeat vitam aeternam. Sic enim Deus dilexit mundum, ut Filiium suum unigenitum daret: ut omnis qui credit in eum, non pereat, sed habeat vitam aeternam. Non enim misit Deus Filium suum in mundum, ut iudicet mundum, sed ut salvetur mundus per ipsum.*"

²⁶It is interesting to note that, whereas the text of Numbers 21: 4-9 was not an explicit part of the liturgy of the Triumph of the Cross in the Middle Ages, it is now the first reading in the modern lectionary of this feast in the Roman Church–precisely because of its direct association with the Johannine text. The second reading in today's liturgy, Philippians 2: 5-11, was actually the first reading in the medieval liturgy. Given Celano's classical education, the resonances between the text from Numbers and John's Gospel would have been obvious and extraordinarily evocative. Cf. Augustine, *Sermo 6*, in CCSL 41 (Turnhout: Brepols, 1961), pp. 65-66.

journey, ⁵the people complained against God and Moses: "Why have you brought us up from Egypt to die in this desert, where there is no food or water? We are disgusted with this wretched food!" ⁶In punishment, the Lord sent among the people *saraph serpents*, which bit the people so that many of them died. ⁷Then the people came to Moses and said: "We have sinned in complaining against the Lord and you. Pray the Lord to take the *serpents* from us." So Moses prayed for the people, ⁸and the Lord said to Moses: "Make a *saraph* and mount it on a pole, and if anyone who has been bitten looks on it, he will recover." ⁹Moses accordingly made a *bronze serpent* and mounted it on a pole, and whenever anyone who had been bitten by a *serpent* looked at the *bronze serpent* that person recovered.[27]

The text tells the story of the grumbling of the Israelites on their way through the wilderness to the Promised Land and of God's sending of "saraph serpents" (*igniti serpentes*) that bite and poison the people. Now these "saraph serpents" or, literally, "fiery snakes" are those snakes whose bites–and the venom which they inject into their victims–produce a fiery, burning sensation.[28] Hence, these snakes represent a destructive, malevolent force in nature. But the serpent was also a symbol in Egypt of power, strength and deliverance from harm;

---

[27]Numbers 21: 4-9: "*Profecti sunt autem de monte Hor, per viam quae ducit ad mare Rubrum, ut circumirent terram Edom. Et taedere coepit populum itineris ac laboris: locutusque contra Deum et Moysen, ait: Cur eduxisti nos de Aegypto, ut moreremur in solitudine? Deest panis, non sunt aquae: anima nostra iam nauseat super cibo isto levissimo. Quamobrem misit Dominus in populum **ignitos serpentes**, ad quorum plagas et mortes plurimorum, venerunt ad Moysen, atque dixerunt: Peccavimus, quia locuti sumus contra Dominum et te: ora ut tollat a nobis **serpentes**. Oravitque Moyses pro populo, et locutus est Dominus ad eum: Fac **serpentem aeneum**, et pone eum pro signo: qui percussus aspexerit eum, vivet. Fecit ergo Moyses **serpentem aeneum**, et posuit eum pro signo: quem cum percussi aspicerent, sanabantur.*"

[28]Hence the use of particular words used in Latin to describe the phenomenon. The Latin word used to describe the serpent that Moses is to mount on a pole is *aeneus* which can be translated both as "brazen" (as in burning) and "bronze" (as in the melting process used to create the metal). Hence, "saraph," "brazen" and "bronze" all refer to the same reality of snakes whose bites burn.

as such, replicas were often mounted on the headdress of the pharaohs in order to project stability, health, well-being and salvation to the people.[29]

Indeed, the prevalence of such snakes in Egypt and their multi-layered significance as symbols of both harm and healing, blessing and curse, are well known. Thus it is not all that surprising that, in a marvelous example of "sympathetic magic," Moses is instructed to fashion and lift up in the sight of the Hebrews a saraph serpent as the symbol–in the very moment of their despair–of their eventual deliverance.[30]

More important, however, is the fact that, in Hebrew, the English words "saraph" and "seraph" would be exactly the same word: שׂרף.[31] Indeed, this identification of "saraph" and "seraph" is clearly seen in two other texts that are found in the book of the prophet Isaiah. The

---

[29]Cf., for example, Manfred Lurker, *The Gods and Symbols of Ancient Egypt: An Illustrated Dictionary* (London: Thames and Hudson, 1980), 125; and Richard H. Wilkinson, *The Complete Gods and Goddesses of Ancient Egypt* (London: Thames and Hudson, 2003), 226-27.

[30]Cf., for example, the illuminating pages of John D. Currid, *Ancient Egypt and the Old Testament* (Grand Rapids, Michigan: Baker Books, 1997), 146-49, passim: "Reacting to the last grumbling incident before the Hebrews reached the Promised Land, God sent them *hannĕḥāšîm haśśĕrāphîm* ("fiery serpents") upon them because of their unfaithfulness. The *nĕḥāšîm* bit many of the Hebrews and some died. Yahweh then ordered Moses to fashion a *śārāph* and set it on a standard or pole in the middle of the Israelite camp. So Moses crafted a *nĕḥaš nĕḥōšet* ("bronze serpent"), and whoever had been bitten needed only to look at the image to be healed. . . .Clearly, the biblical writer employed Egyptian background material and motifs when recording the Numbers 21 incident. . . .But . . . [w]hy the Egyptian symbol of a bronze serpent? First of all, this episode is an example of sympathetic magic, that is, 'controlling an adversary through manipulation of a replication.' Moses and the Israelites attempted to change curse into blessing by manipulating an image of the very thing bringing the curse. . . . In summary, the construction of the bronze serpent signified blessing and curse. Those Hebrews who were bitten by the fiery serpents needed only to look to the bronze serpent and they would be healed. That was the blessing. However, the brass image also symbolized the destruction of Egypt . . . and of those who wished to return to Egypt and her ways. That was the curse." On the issue of sympathetic magic, Currid is quoting T.E. Fretheim, "Life in the Wilderness," *Dialog* 17 (1978): 267.

[31]One must recall that there are no written vowels in Hebrew. I would like to thank Prof. Michael Calabria (St. Bonaventure University) for his generous assistance with the Hebrew language.

first text is Isaiah 14: 29. Although the actual content of the passage is rather obscure, requiring an appreciation of the context of the prophetic allusion and his use of symbolic language to understand the image, the identification of saraphs/seraphs with snakes is quite clear:

> Rejoice not, O Philistia, not one of you that the rod which smote you is broken: for out of the serpent's root will come an adder, its fruit shall be a ***flying saraph***.[32]

The serpent's offspring is thus identified as a saraph/seraph. But one new element has now been added to the description: it is a saraph that flies. In other words, it is a fiery snake that has wings.[33]

Now, this same fascinating detail also appears in an earlier passage in the book of the prophet Isaiah 6: 1-3:

> ¹In the year King Uzziah died, I saw the Lord seated on a high and lofty throne, with the train of his garment filling the temple. ²***Seraphim*** were stationed above; each of them had six wings: with two they veiled their faces, with two they veiled their feet, and with two they hovered aloft. ³"Holy, holy, holy, is the Lord of hosts!" they cried one to the other. "All the earth is filled with his glory!"[34]

---

[32] Isa 14:29: "*Ne laeteris, Philisthaea, omnis tu, quoniam comminute est virga percussoris tui; de radice enim colubri egredietur regulus, et semen eius **absorbens volucrem*** [Hebrew: שָׂרָף]."

[33] Again the comments of J.D. Currid (146, note 16) on the identification of saraphs with snakes are relevant: "Isa. 14:29 and 30:6. There is no uncertainty that the prophet has a snake in view because *śārāph mě ʿôpēp* is parallel with 'viper' in both of these instances. A similar parallel is found in the later writings of Herodotus . . . [who] also connects flying serpents to Egypt: 'The trees which bear frankincense [in Arabia] are guarded by winged serpents, small in size and of varied colors, whereof vast numbers hang about every tree. They are of the same kind as the serpents which invade Egypt.'" See also: D.J. Wiseman, "Flying Serpents," *Tyndale Bulletin* 23 (1972): 108-10.

[34] Isa 6:1-3: "*In anno quo mortuus est rex Ozias, vidi Dominum sedentem super solium excelsum et elevatum; et ea quae sub ipso erant replebant templum.* **Seraphim** [Hebrew: שְׂרָפִים] *stabant super illud: sex alae uni, et sex alae alteri; duabus velabant faciem ius, et duabus velabant pedes eius, et duabus volabant. Et clamabant alter ad alterum, et dicebant: Sanctus, sanctus, sanctus Dominus Deus exercituum; plena est omnis terra gloria eius.*"

There are two details to notice here. First, once again the saraph/seraph–that is to say, the fiery snake–has wings, just as it did in Isaiah 14: 29. In fact, it has six wings: two above, two below and two for flight. And second, this particular passage uses the word "saraph" now in its plural form: *saraphim* or, as we are more used to seeing it rendered, *seraphim*.[35]

These associations are clear and unmistakable in the Hebrew. However, were they as evident in the Latin? A comparison of the Vulgate translation of the account in Numbers 21: 4-9 would reveal that the Latin vocabulary does not convey the same resonances and assonances with the Hebrew and English vocabulary, as would be evident to scholars today. The question is: would anyone have appreciated the association of the seraphic language of Isaiah 14: 29 and 6: 1-3 with the saraphs/seraphs of Numbers 21: 4-9 (and, by extension, with John 3: 13-17)? This is the most difficult and the most pivotal question; and it is one that requires a definitive response–one that unfortunately cannot yet be given. However, for the response to be in the affirmative, such a person would either had to have known Hebrew or, more probably, had to have known Latin works that were aware of the resonances.[36] We have seen that the connection between the allusion to Moses in the Gospel of John and his actions in the

---

[35] Cf. J.D. Currid (p. 146): "The Hebrew word *sārāph* appears only seven times in the Old Testament, and each occurrence signifies some kind of snake. . . .Apparently the *naḥas śārāph* was a common creature in the desert areas of Sinai. Isaiah 6 represents the attendants of Yahweh as *seraphim* with six wings, and elsewhere the prophet speaks of *śārāph meʕopēp* ("a fiery flying one"). By definition, 'a saraph is a serpent, and for Isaiah it may have wings, as is the case with the seraphim of Isaiah 6.'" Currid is quoting an article by K.R. Joines, "Winged Serpents in Isaiah's Inaugural Vision," *Journal of Biblical Literature* 86 (1967): 411.

[36] An obvious source would have been Isidore of Seville's *Etymologies*. However, his comments in Part VII, c. V, 24-25: *De angelis*, on the meaning of the word "Seraphim" do not attest to these resonances: "*Seraphin quoque similiter multitudo est angelorum, qui ex Hebraeo in Latinum ardentes vel incendentes interpretantur. Qui idcirco ardentes vocantur, quia inter eos et Deum nulli angeli consistunt; et ideo quanto vicinius coram eo consistunt, tanto magis luminis claritate divini inflammantur. Unde et ipsi velant faciem et pedes sedentis in throno Dei; et idcirco cetera angelorum turba videre Dei essentiam plene non valent, quoniam Cherubin eam tegit.*"

Book of Numbers was a fairly standard association.[37] At this stage of our research, we can only state that the conjunction of the saraphs/seraphs in the desert of the Book of Numbers, the allusion to the lifting up of the saraph/seraph on the pole in John and the use of the image of the saraph/seraph in the first narrative account of the stigmatization in the *Vita prima*, is simply too evocative to be ignored. Indeed, as we will see, it goes a long way toward explaining what Celano was trying to describe might have happened to Francis in this most intense moment of prayer.

Given these saraphic images and their unexpected associations with fiery snakes that have wings, are we thus to assume that Celano is telling us in his account that Francis was "seeing" or contemplating a snake . . . rather than an angel? Not entirely.

We must ask two further questions. First, where does the identification of the content of the vision on La Verna with the saraphic imagery come from? And second, what is this identification supposed to mean?

As to the first question, does the identification come from Francis himself? Most probably not: Francis had an experience–a mystical experience–the contents and meaning of which, by all accounts, he kept to himself. Indeed, all of our authors seem to go out of their way to repeatedly tell us that he did not talk about the experience, implying that the imagery used is theirs, not his.

But if it does not originate with Francis, then is it Leo who makes the association? Leo was, after all, on La Verna with Francis and, at least by the testimony of the *Actus beati Francisci*, seems to have been fairly physically proximate to Francis at the time of these events. Moreover, on the back side of the *chartula*, in his first and most extensive explication of the events surrounding the writing of this tiny piece of parchment, Leo clearly states:

> Two years before his death, the blessed Francis spent forty days on Mount La Verna from the Feast of the Assumption of the holy Virgin Mary until the September Feast of Saint

---

[37]Cf. above, note 26.

Michael, in honor of the Blessed Virgin Mary, the Mother of God, and blessed Michael the Archangel. And the Lord's hand was upon him. After the vision and message of the **Seraph** and the impression of Christ's stigmata upon his body, he composed these praises written on the other side of this page and wrote them in his own hand, thanking God for the kindness bestowed on him.[38]

Note that Leo uses the phrase "vision and message of the Seraph" to describe the experience of Francis. However, is the use of the term "Seraph" original to him? This text, we know, is quite late, having been written most probably at some time in the 1260s. Indeed, once he had gained possession of the *chartula* after the events on La Verna, Leo apparently folded it over (into fours) and carried it around with him, possibly draped over the cord of his habit, almost as a kind of talisman, for it contained upon it a precious blessing written explicitly for him by his beloved Francis.[39] Furthermore, we now know that these Leonine explications–there are three of them on the backside of the parchment–were added rather late in his life. For whereas the outside (that is to say, the front side of the *chartula* containing the *Praises of God*) has been virtually obliterated from years of wear and tear (having become the outer side of the document), the verso (or back side) containing the blessing, the Tau and the mysterious head are all still in relatively good shape. And it is on this side, in three open areas on the page–on the very top of the parchment, in an area across the middle of the page, and then at the very bottom–that Leo wrote in red

---

[38] *Benedictio fratri Leoni data*: "*Beatus Franciscus duobus annis ante mortem suam fecit quadragesimam in loco Alvernae ad honorem beatae Virginis, matris Dei, et beati Michaelis archangeli a festo assumptionis sanctae Mariae virginis usque ad festum sancti Michaelis septembris; et facta est super eum manus Domini; post visionem et allocutionem Seraphim et impressionem stigmatum Christi in corpore suo fecit has laudes ex alio latere chartulae scriptas et manu sua scripsit gratias agens Deo de beneficio sibi collato.*" Hereafter, cited as BenLeo.

[39] See the description of this in: A. Bartoli Langeli, *Gli autografi di frate Francesco e di frate Leone*, Corpus Christianorum. Autographa Medii Aevi, 5 (Turnhout: Brepols, 2000), 30-44, esp. p. 30. The description of the *chartula* by John V. Fleming in *From Bonaventure to Bellini: An Essay in Franciscan Exegesis* (Princeton: Princeton University Press, 1982), 99-106 is based on its depiction by the artist Bellini.

middle of the page, and then at the very bottom–that Leo wrote in red ink his three explications. The fact that these are in much better shape than anything else on the verso side of the *chartula* shows that they must have been added to the document, probably not before 1260: in short, some time closer to his own death, between 1260 and 1271.[40]

Therefore, Leo's use of the term ***seraphim*** is late. However, while not totally excluding that the use of the image of the seraph might have originated with him (or another companion who had been with Francis on La Verna), a much simpler and more credible explanation is certainly available to us: namely, that it comes from Thomas of Celano himself, author of the first narrative account in the *Vita prima*. All other authors who wrote on the matter–Julian of Speyer, Henri d'Avranches, the author of the *Three Companions*, Bonaventure, even Leo himself–simply take over the imagery used by the official hagiographer in this first foundational account. It becomes, in other words, the classic account of the event and its imagery the standard manner of describing an unknown (if not unknowable) experience.

Indeed, in drafting the first narrative of the event, it is Thomas who explicitly chooses to use the image from Isaiah 6: 2–the text we examined earlier–to describe what Francis was seeing or experiencing in the stigmatization vision in which a man "like a saraph [or seraph]" with six wings is perceived as hovering above him. The question is: why does he choose this particular text of Isaiah? To assert that the hagiographer was simply borrowing the veiled allusions to the image of the seraph evoked by Gregory IX in his bull of canonization for Francis, *Mirca circa nos*, is not enough by itself; such allusions do not explain the significant development of the content and meaning of the experience now found in the narrative. No, the answer lies elsewhere.

---

[40]Cf. my comments on the possible connection between Leo's testimony and Bonaventure's account of the stigmatization, above, note 22. One wonders what the motivation for these explications might have been. What is simply for posterity's sake that Leo felt that he needed to explain what he knew about the parchment? Or was he trying to convey information to someone in particular? Is it possible that it had some connection to Bonaventure's visit to the area around 1260 in order to gather information from the surviving companions? It would be interesting and perhaps revelatory to know the context for the added rubrics.

Thomas would have heard the testimony of those friars who had seen the body of their founder after his death. He would also have known what Elias had written in his encyclical letter, boldly affirming that Francis had "appeared crucified, bearing in his body the five wounds."[41] And finally, he would have been keenly aware of the bull of canonization wherein Gregory likewise described Francis's flesh as having been "crucified."[42] Nevertheless, it is Celano who takes it upon himself to go one step further: to link the *wounds* of the Crucified with an *experience of* the Crucified. And that experience, for Celano, was inescapably and indelibly linked with a profound meditation upon the cross of Jesus Christ.[43]

Celano, in other words, must have surmised that what Francis on La Verna was meditating upon was the cross of Christ depicted so powerfully, for example, in the text of the gospel of John 3 or possibly even–though less graphically–in the text of the gospel of John 12. Indeed, Celano is less concerned with the day upon which this might have occurred as he is about the text and the prayer which might have

---

[41]*Epistola encyclica*, AF 10, p. 526, n. 5: "Et his dictis, annuntio *vobis gaudium magnum* et miraculi novitatem. *A saeculo non est auditum* tale *signum*, praeterquam *in Filio Dei, qui est Christus Dominus*. Non diu ante mortem frater et pater noster apparuit crucifixus, quinque plagas, quae vere sunt *stigmata Christi, portans in corpore suo*. . . ." The italicized words are allusions to scriptural passages.

[42]*Mira circa nos*, BF I, p. 43: "*Et in Terram visionis accedens, super unum sibi montium demonstratum . . . qua cum vitiis, et concupiscentiis crucifixa* [cf. Gal 5:24], *dicere portat cum Apostolo: 'Vivo ego, iam non ego, vivit eum in me Christus'* [Gal 2: 20]."

[43]The aforementioned article of Jacques Dalarun posits that Celano probably borrowed the allusion to the Seraph from Gregory IX's bull of canonization, *Mira circa nos*. That allusion makes reference backward to a text of Bernard of Clairvaux (*Sermones in Cantica canticorum*, 19,5 in PL 183, p. 865) who, likewise, was borrowing a classic association already made by Gregory the Great (*Homilia in Evangelia*, XXXIV, n. 14, in CCSL 112: 313-14: "*Seraphim namque incendium diximus, et tamen amore conditoris simul omnes ardent*"). However, the context in all three texts is an asceticism undertaken for the love of God. If Celano had caught the allusion made by Gregory IX to these classic texts– and he almost assuredly did–he then went on to radically change the orientation of the traditional allusion from asceticism (crucifying his flesh through ascetical practices) to something else. For Celano will transform the allusion from an ascetical mastery of his flesh out of love for God into an account of a profound meditation upon the cross of Christ in which his own flesh is transformed not by ascetical acts but by the experience of prayer itself. The question is, *why* does Celano develop the original allusion–and *how*?

prompted the ecstatic experience.[44] Moreover, it is Thomas–and not Francis–who would have known of the resonances between the image of the cross lifted up for the healing and salvation of the world and the more explicit account of Numbers 21 which mentions the saraph serpents: those fiery snakes whose bronze replicas would bring healing to all who looked upon them. But again: it is not a snake that Francis would have been contemplating during his mystical transport. Rather, what Francis is seeing in ecstasy–and what Celano is trying to render in language that unites no less than three biblical accounts (John 3, Numbers 21 and Isaiah 6)–is the figure of Jesus Christ lifted up on the cross for the healing and salvation of the world. For just as Moses lifted up the saraph serpent in the desert so that all who looked upon it would find healing, now Francis, in contemplating Christ lifted up on the cross, was being assured of the ultimate healing and salvation of the world promised in Christ crucified.

---

[44]Hence, it seems to me, the absence of a specific time-reference in 1 Cel 92-94. Given our close examination thus far of the content of the first texts that deal with the stigmatization of Francis, I would summarize the development of events in the following manner: (1) the experience of the stigmatization (September, 1224); (2) the public announcement of its occurrence in the 1226 encyclical letter of Brother Elias upon the death of Francis; (3) Gregory IX's 1228 association of the marks of the stigmata with a life-long and intense asceticism by Francis (crucifying his flesh out of love for God), with a veiled allusion to the Seraph–the symbol *par excellence* of ardent, burning love; (4) in 1229, Celano's critical transposition of this experience from the realm of asceticism to that of mysticism, now directly associated with Francis's meditation upon the cross of the Crucified Christ, who is identified explicitly with the image of the Seraph; and lastly (5) the association of Francis's profound meditation on the cross (and thus the event of the stigmatization) with the Feast of the Exaltation of the Cross ("on or about the feast") in 1246 by the author of the Legend of the Three Companions. Hence, the identification of which Gospel was actually used on the feast becomes somewhat secondary; what is crucial is what **Celano** thought Francis was meditating on–the cross of Christ–and how he chose to dramatize that. The *Vita prima* is thus the critical link between *Mira circa nos* and 3 Soc in two ways: through his identification of the experience with a meditation upon the cross of the Crucified and through his imaginative, even ground-breaking use of the seraphic imagery (from John, Numbers and Isaiah) in order to try to **explain** that experience. No one had until then made such an explicit identification of the saraph/seraph with the cross of Christ (except, of course, the Gospel of John itself). It was the event of the stigmatization and Celano's desire to understand it from within that prompted him, it seems to me, to boldly cross this threshold.

A close reading of both 1 Celano and Bonaventure shows quite clearly that what Francis was seeing was "a *man* . . . affixed to a cross" (Celano) and "a *man* crucified in the midst of the wings . . . nailed to a cross" (Bonaventure).[45] In other words, the saraph/seraph is not really a snake at all: it is a man. And that man is Jesus Christ. Thomas chooses to use the vehicle of the imagery of the seraph (the winged seraph)– cited textually from Isaiah 6:2 but evoking Numbers 21–in order to convey the mystical experience of Francis, meditating upon Christ on the cross. What Francis saw *above* him–and Celano knew this–was not an angel but Christ: lifted up, *spatially above him*, on the cross for the healing of the human race. Thomas, in other words, different from Gregory IX in his bull *Mira circa nos*, was striving to get **inside** the experience of Francis: to understand what might have produced or generated the mysterious marks on the body of Francis and to grapple with the implications of such an event. This is what separates him from the classic images of asceticism used by Gregory IX. They may indeed have had the image of the Seraphim in common (veiled in *Mirca circa nos*, now explicit in the *Vita prima*). But it is Thomas who relates the experience directly to the cross, using highly symbolic, biblical language and aided by an awareness of the context of Francis's experience on La Verna: his prayer centered on the exaltation of Christ on the cross.

Note that Thomas never says it was an angel that Francis saw. Indeed, he never uses the word *angelus* in his account at all. As the *Instrumentum de stigmatibus beati Francisci* has Francis himself relate it in a vision to a pious lay brother: **"*Nam ille qui mihi tunc apparuit, non fuit Angelus, sed Dominus Iesus Christus in specie Seraphim.*"**[46]

---

[45] 1 Cel 94: ". . . *vidit in visione Dei virum unum, quasi Seraphim sex alas habentem . . .*"; LMaj XIII:3: ". . . *vidit Seraph unum sex alas habentem, tam ignitas quam splendidas . . . apparuit inter alas effigies hominis crucifixi, in modum cruces manus et pedes extensos habentis et cruci affixos.*"

[46] It is interesting that this issue was a also question among certain friars in the thirteenth century. In the *Instrumentum de stigmatibus beati Francisci* (pp. 644-46), the following testimony from 1282 is reported: "*Anno Domini MCCLXXXII, V. nonas Octobris, ego frater Philippus, Minister Thusciae, volens exsequi mandatum quoddam mihi factum a venerabili patre fratre Bonagratia, Ministro Generali Ordinis fratrum Minorum, in generali capitulo eodem anno Argentinae celebrato, ut scilicet investigarem diligentius diem et*

We moderns are the ones who tend to conflate the image of the Seraph with an angel, and then project our own conflation onto the iconographical representations, which can indeed seem to convey a similar identification. But medieval personages, more sensitive and accustomed to the use of symbolic language, were generally able to hold the two images together–the man Christ and a seraphic figure–both literally as well as artistically, even to the point of producing some seemingly awkward iconographical representations (e.g., a man nailed to a cross enfolded within the wings of a Seraph).

However, what seems to happen over the course of time is that as Thomas' brilliant use of biblical symbolism moves forward through the thirteenth and fourteenth centuries, especially as it comes to be read through the lens–if not the actual language–of Bonaventure and into

---

horam, qua sacra stigmata corpori beati Francisci fuerint impressa, fratrem unum laicum mirae pietatis et vitae probatissimae, cui audieram revelationem aliquam esse de hoc factam, habui in mea praesentia et exegi ab eo, ut mihi circa hoc omnem panderet veritatem.

Ipse igitur humili animo et pura intentione respondit, quod rogatus olim multa instantia a fratre Iohanne de Castellione Aretii Custodiae, ut apud beatum Franciscum intercederet, quatenus sibi diem et horam, quando beato Francisco stigmata fuerint impressa, revelaret. Acquiescens eius precum instantiae, anno praeterito MCCLXXXI in mense Maio, cum ad locum Alvernae de speciali mea licentia accessisset, in cella, quae in loco illo, ubi apparitio facta esse dicitur, constructa est, [ad] orationem se contulit nocte quadam die Veneris illucescente suppliciter postulans, ut Deus personae alicui hoc revelaret. . . .

. . . Quo respiciente versus introitum cellae, ecce beatus Pater Franciscus astitit ante ipsum et dixit illi Latinis verbis: 'Fili, quid facis tu hic?' At ipse voce tacitus affectione cordis suum des-iderium de praefata revelatione depromebat. Iterum eum beatus Pater vulgaribus verbis alloquitur dicens: 'De quo rogas tu Deum, ut debeat revelare tibi?' Tunc frater voce respondit dicens: 'Pater, rogabam Deum, ut dignaretur revelare, qua die et hora tibi sacra stigmata fuerunt impressa.' Tunc sanctus Pater dixit ei: 'Deus vult, ut scias tu, et ego dicam tibi. Ego enim sum pater vester Franciscus et bene me nosti;' et ostendit stigmata manuum et pedum et lateris addens, 'quod tempus adest, quod Deus propalare vult, quod fratres hactenus neglexerunt. **Nam ille qui mihi tunc apparuit, non fuit Angelus, sed Dominus Iesus Christus in specie Seraphim,** *qui sicut vulnera ipsa sacra in cruce positus suo corpore suscepit, ita ea manibus suis corpori meo impressit.' Modum autem apparitionis describens beatus Pater adiecit: 'Proxima die ante festum Exaltationis sanctae Crucis venit ad me unus Angelus dicens mihi ex parte Dei, quod me ad patientiam et ad recipiendum quod in me Deus vellet facere, praepararem. . . .In mane ergo diei Exaltationis sanctae Crucis summo diluculo exiens cellam in vehementissimo fervore spiritus ad locum quendam orationi solitum properabam. Et ecce per aëra iuvenis quidam crucifixus praeferens speciem Seraphim sex alas habentis cum magno impetu descendebat. . . .'"*

the modern era, the original multi-layered and evocative account of Celano comes to be eclipsed if not entirely lost from view.[47] Indeed, it must be recalled that it is the *Legenda maior* and not the *Vita prima* which for centuries will serve as the primary formative text for the life and meaning of Francis. Moreover, given the critical importance of the angelic hierarchies in Bonaventure's theological writings, thoroughly absorbed from Pseudo-Dionysius and the Victorine theologians of the previous century, it is not surprising that the saraphic/seraphic imagery in his monumental *legenda* comes to be read not as the fiery winged snakes in the Book of Numbers or the prophet Isaiah but rather as the angelic imagery of the New Testament, especially in the Pauline letters.

Hence, we elide from snakes to angels and, in so doing, we lose sight of Christ, the crucified man lifted up on the cross. In other words, the winged snake of the Old Testament will be conceptualized more and more as a winged angel from the New Testament–thereby losing the power of the original ecstatic experience of Francis. What is eclipsed is Celano's profound association of the event of the stigmatization with Francis's contemplation of Christ raised up on the cross through a reflection upon a text like John 3 on or around the feast of

---

[47]Such a reading, however, need not have a Bonaventurean causation. All that was required was the simple conflation of the Old Testament image of the seraph with that of an angel. The account given in Thomas of Eccleston [*Tractatus de adventu in fratrum minorum in Angliam*, ed. A.G. Little (Manchester: Manchester University Press, 1951), 75] is indicative of such a conflation. He reports the testimony of a provincial minister of England, Peter of Tewkesbury, who claims to have heard from Leo himself a report of the event on La Verna. Notice the language: "*Sed et frater Leo, socius sancti Francisci, dixit fratri Petro, ministro Angliae, quod apparitio Seraphyn facta fuit sancto Francisco in quodam raptu contemplationis, et satis evidentius, quam scribatur in vita sua; et quod multa fuerunt tunc sibi revelata, quae nulli viventi unquam communicavit. Verumtamen dixit fratri Ruffino socio suo, quod, cum a longe videret **angelum**, nimis territus fuit, et quod eum dure tractavit; et dixit ei, quod ordo suus duraret usque ad finem mundi, et nullus malae voluntatis diu durare possit in ordine, et quod nullus odiens ordinem diu viveret, et quod nullus veraciter amans ordinem suum malum finem haberet. Praecepit autem sanctus Franciscus fratri Rufino, ut lapidem, super quem steterat **angelus**, lavaret et ungeret oleo; quod et fecit. Ista scripsit frater Garynus de Sedenefeld ab ore fratris Leonis.*" The assumption is that the Seraph *was* an angel–an identification that was refuted, as we have seen, by the testimony in the *Instrumentum de stigmatibus beati Francisci*" (cf. above, note 46).

the Exaltation of the Cross. Instead, we are left with the impression that what Francis was seeing in this event was a strange fluttering angel with a surplus of wings.

But our recovery of the original association has more profound, even radical, implications. For if indeed it is not an angel or an angelic presence that hovers above Francis during that momentous day on La Verna, then we are in a much better position to appreciate the extraordinary depth of the actual experience. Rather than conceive of the stigmatization of Francis as an event whereby an angelic figure literally zaps something *onto* Francis from the outside (an impression that can indeed be conveyed in medieval and renaissance artistic representations of the event), we can now begin to appreciate that the stigmatization was, in fact, something that came from deep within him and out of him, onto his very flesh. The trajectory of the experience, in other words, was not from the outside-in but rather from the inside-out. Indeed, Celano's own description of the wounds-marks that begin appear on his body shortly after the experience clearly describes skin that is protruding outward rather than something that has been pushed inward into him.[48]

For in truth, at least from a post-Enlightenment perspective, angels do not go around hovering above people and zapping them. However, profound, intense, even mystical prayer can begin to literally explode out of one's psyche (one's soul) into and through one's very flesh, when the object of one's prayer–like Christ nailed to the cross–has been so thoroughly interiorized. This is the deepest and most authentic form of a psychosomatic event: not in the sense of something fraudulently induced but of something that comes up out of the very depths of one's being, manifesting its effects in one's own body. We

---

[48] 1 Cel 95: "*Manus et pedes eius in ipso medio clavis confixae videbantur, clavorum capitibus in interiore parte manuum et superiore pedum apparentibus, et eorum acuminibus exsistentibus ex adverso. Erant enim signa illa rotunda interius in manibus, exterius autem oblonga, et caruncula quaedam apparebat quasi summitas clavorum retorta et repercussa, quae carnem reliquam excedebat. Sic et in pedibus impressa erant signa clavorum et a carne reliqua elevata. . . .*" LMaj XIII:3: "*. . . erantque clavorum capita in manibus et pedibus rotunda et nigra, ipsa vero acumina oblonga, retorta et quasi repercussa, quae de ipsa carne surgentia carnem reliquam excedebant. . . .*"

are, in other words, in the presence of a breathtaking and awesome experience of human prayer at its most intense, where grace and nature have become so commingled through the medium of a meditation upon Christ's passion. Brother Elias was probably not far from the truth in calling the result of this commingling the *novitas miraculi*: not in the sense that nature has been contravened but rather in the sense that what appears on Francis's body–*in* Francis's body–has become a sign of God's deepest *conversatio* with the human person. Perhaps, therefore, Bonaventure's theological insight–namely, that Francis actually bore the stigmata (that is, the cross of Christ) within himself from the very moment of his conversion and that it gradually deepened and intensified until it emerged onto his flesh on La Verna–is not very far from the truth of the mystical experience of Francis in September 1224.

Part II: The Chartula of St. Francis and its Relationship to the Event of the Stigmatization of Francis of Assisi

We now need to ask: *why* did this meditation upon Christ, lifted up for the healing and salvation of the human race, have such a profound impact upon Francis during his time of prayer on La Verna? It is this second part of the story which sheds light on that question. For that we turn to examine the famous *chartula* of St. Francis.

Brother Leo tells us, in the text from the *chartula* cited earlier,[49] that after Francis had received the stigmata, he wrote on the *recto* (front) side of the parchment a prayer called *The Praises of God*.[50] However, it is the *verso* (back) side of the *chartula* that needs to be the focus of our attention. This verso side is actually quite familiar to many, appearing as it does on any number of reproductions of Franciscan art and iconography. In fact, this tiny piece of parchment is

---

[49]See the text cited above, note 38.
[50]"Laudes Dei altissimi," Kajetan Esser, *Die Opuscula des hl. Franziskus von Assisi: Neue textkritische Edition*, Spicilegium Bonaventurianum, 13 (Grottaferrata: Editiones Collegii S. Bonaventurae, 1976), 142.

quite small, measuring approximately 5½" (height) x 4" (width). But how precious indeed is this miniscule document![51]

The back side actually comprises five different or distinguishable parts. If one were to separate them out, it would look something like this:

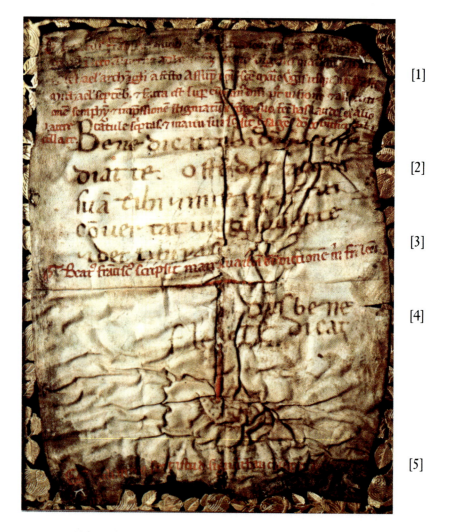

[1]

[2]

[3]

[4]

[5]

---

[51]A brief description of the parchment is given in: A. Bartoli Langeli, *Gli autografi*, 30.

[1] Leo's First Explication (in red ink): an account of the events on La Verna.

[2] The Blessing of Aaron from Numbers 6:24-26:

> *May the Lord bless and keep you;*
> *May he show his face to you and be merciful to you;*
> *May he turn his countenance to you and give you peace.*[52]

[3] Leo's Second Explication (in red): that Francis wrote a blessing for him.[53]

[4] A Tau cross (drawn over in red):

- at the base of which appears to be a recumbent head looking upward;
- surrounded by (or placed within or beneath) a jagged outline;
- with words written under the right arm of the Tau;[54]
- and a word or words across the shaft of the Tau;[55]

[5] Leo's Third Explication (in red): that Francis drew the Tau and head.[56]

---

[52] BenLeo: "*Benedicat tibi Dominus et custodiat te; ostendat faciem suam tibi et misereatur tui. Convertat vultum suum ad te et det tibi pacem* [Nm 6: 24-26]."

[53] BenLeo: "*Beatus Franciscus scripsit manu sua istam benedictionem mihi fratri Leoni.*"

[54] BenLeo: "*Dominus benedicat*" (or possibly "*Dominus bene dicat*"). The placement of these words has been, of course, the subject of much debate and speculation. A. Bartoli Langeli (*Autografi*, 40) gives an approximate positioning of the letters in his chapter on the *chartula*; as does Duane Lapsanski, "The Autographs on the 'Chartula' of St. Francis of Assisi," *AFH* 67 (1974): 34. Most helpful in this regard–because it illustrates the precise relationship of the words to the Tau–is the diagram in the article of John V. Fleming, "The Iconographic Unity of the Blessing for Brother Leo, *Franziskanische Studien* 63 (1981): 207.

[55] BenLeo: f le(T)o te. I will address the difficult problem of how these letters might be read a little further on in the article.

[56] BenLeo: "*Simili modo fecit istud signum thau cum capite manu sua.*"

Now this *verso* side of the *chartula* has posed numerous problems for interpreters as to whether they comprise a unified whole or, if not, what the separate parts might actually mean.

The three explications in red of Leo are fairly easy to interpret: they are the statements added later by Leo who felt the need to give an accounting of the content of the back side of the *chartula*. For whom, we do not know for certain, although I have conjectured earlier that it may have been connected in some way with Bonaventure's visit to central Italy and his questioning of the surviving companions in preparation for his drafting of the *Legenda maior*.[57] However, Leo does not so much *explain* what is there as simply *state* what is on the parchment. And therein lies part of the dilemma for interpreters; we are left to puzzle out the relationship–if any–between the various parts. Hence, I am first going to attempt to explain, in summary fashion, the meaning of sections [2] and [4]–that is, the Aaronic blessing and the four elements comprising the Tau: the mysterious head, the jagged outline surrounding the head, and the enigmatic writing. Then, in the conclusion of the article, I will relate these findings to the experience of the stigmata.

There are two keys to unraveling the meaning of this *verso* side of the *chartula*: (1) one must be able to explain the strange head that appears at the base of the Tau; and (2) one must be able to explain–or at least offer a reasonable hypothesis that coheres with the first explanation–the words that appear underneath the right arm of the Tau and those that intersect the shaft of the Tau.[58] This is no small task. Several historians of note have attempted to explain the latter issue–with varying results. A few others have conjectured about the possible identification and significance of the mysterious head, without a

---

[57]See above, note 22.

[58]On the Tau, see, for example, Damien Vorreux, *Un symbole franciscain: le Tau*, 2 ed. (Paris: Éditions franciscaines, 1996); and, more generally, Karl Rahner, "*Antenna cruces* V, Das mystische Tau," *Zeitschrift für Katholische Theologie* 75 (1953): 385-410.

convincing rationale or satisfactory demonstration. At this stage in my own research on the matter and for our purposes here, I will concentrate primarily on the first issue (the identification of the head), while touching on the issues raised by the second without attempting a definitive explanation of the matter.

The key to the solution of the meaning of the verso side of the *chartula* pivots on how one interprets the mysterious head lying recumbent at the foot of the Tau. There are two main lines of interpretation of this enigmatic figure. Several interpreters have speculated that, given the traditional association of Brother Leo to the blessing on the backside of the parchment and the three explications that he added later in life, Francis would have been drawing on this parchment a representation of Leo himself. In this view, Leo is being protected by the Tau, much as the blessing for him above promises: *Benedicat tibi Dominus et custodiat te. . . .*[59] Others have posited, more convincingly, that the head might be the head of Adam and that the Tau represents the cross erected on Calvary where Adam's sin has been reversed through the death of Christ, the New Adam, represented by the Tau/cross.[60] Note,

---

[59]Such is the reading, for example, of scholars like: Montgomery Carmichael, *La benedizione di san Francesco. Spiegazione del geroglifico* (Livorno: Raffaelo Giusti, 1900); S.J.P. van Dijk, "Saint Francis' Blessing of Brother Leo," *Archivum Franciscanum Historicum* 47 (1954): 199-201; Octavian von Rieden, *Das Leiden Christi im Leben des hl. Franziskus von Assisi* (Rome: Istituto Storico dei Fr. Min. Cappuccini, 1960), 20-21; Damien Vorreux, *Un symbole franciscain: le Tau*, 2 ed. (Paris: Éditions franciscaines, 1996), 82; and A. Bartoli Langeli, *Gli autografi*, 31-32.

[60]Notably: Angelo Cresi, "La benedizione di fra Leone scritta da S. Francesco alla Verna," *La Verna* 11 (1913): 110-22, esp. 118-22; Jacques Cambell, "Les écrits de saint François devant la critique," *Franzikanische Studien* 36 (1954): 218-20; Sophronius Classen, "Miszellen zur Geschichte des hl. Franziskus von Assisi," *Wissenschaft und Weisheit* 35 (1972): 217-19; and Duane Lapsanski, "The Autographs on the 'Chartula' of St. Francis of Assisi," *AFH* 67 (1974): 18-37," esp. 33-37. Indeed, Lapsanski (pp. 36-37), on the basis of a transcription of the mysterious figures found in manuscript As1 [= Assisi, Biblioteca Comunale, cod. 344], believes that "the head is the skull of Adam, the father of mankind . . . a graphic representation of an ancient legend . . . [namely] . . . that Christ was crucified on the very spot Adam was buried." The

however, that in these interpretations, the Tau has two different and possible functions: in the first, it is something that protects[61] whereas in the second, it is something that one confesses, since the cross seems to be emerging from the mouth of the head. It will be important in our interpretation to determine which reading is more accurate or appropriate.

I would, however, like to advance a third possible interpretation—one already hinted at by at least one historian who never really explained how this could be and why.[62]

For if one looks very closely at the head,[63] one sees what looks very much like a turban—a three-tiered construction on the top of the recumbent head—as well as, very clearly, a face that is studded with the follicles of a beard. I want to suggest that the mysterious head that has stumped historians and iconographers alike is not only a turbaned Muslim but none other than the head of the Sultan, Malik al-Kamil—the man

---

transcription is reproduced opposite p. 36. But an even finer reproduction is found in A. Cressi, "Benedizione," between pp. 120-21 as *Tavola V*. A much more nuanced, even provocative interpretation is found in the justly famous article by John V. Fleming, "The Iconographic Unity of the Blessing for Brother Leo," *Franziskanische Studien* 63 (1981): 203-20. I will return to Fleming's argument concerning the enigmatic words under the Tau a little further on.

[61]Much like in the Old Testament passage from the book of the prophet Ezekiel (9: 2, 4-6), where the Tau is a mark that shields the righteous from the wrath of God's ministers during the destruction of Jerusalem: "*Et ecce sex viri veniebant de via portae superioris, quae respecit ad aquilonem, et uniuscuiusque vas interitus in manu eius; vir quoque unus in medio eorum vestitus erat lineis, et atramentarium scriptoris ad renes eius. . . . Et dixit Dominus ad eum: Transi per mediam civitatem, in medio Ierusalem, et signa thau super frontes virorum gementium et dolentium super cunctis abominationibus quae fiunt in medio eius. Et illis dixit, audiente me: Transite per civitatem sequentes eum, et percutite; non parcat oculus vester, neque misereamini; senem, adolescentulum et virginem, parvulum et mulieres, interficite usque ad internecionem; omnem autem super quem videritis thau, ne occidatis, et a sanctuario meo incipite. . . .*"

[62]Francis de Beer, *François, que disait-on de toi?* (Paris: Éditions Franciscaines, 1977), 107-10.

[63]*Contra* Lapsanski and others, note that Leo refers to this figure explicitly as a *caput* and not a *cranium*. The difference, however, made be more academic than substantive.

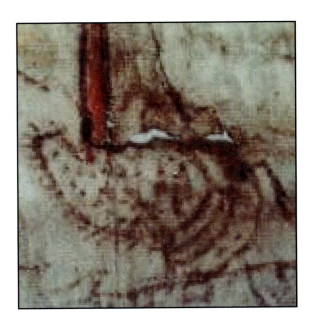

whom Francis had encountered under his tent, in Egypt, in September 1219, immediately after the defeat of the Christian crusaders at Damietta! And the jagged drawing surrounding or circumscribing this recumbent head is neither the mountain of La Verna nor the hill of Calvary but rather a representation of the shores of the Mediterranean Sea with the turban touching the approximate location of Damietta in Egypt, the place of their encounter.

The question is: why would the head of the Sultan be on a *Blessing to Brother Leo*? Why indeed!

What has rarely, if ever, been noticed is that, in April, 1223, Pope Honorius III had recently announced that a new military venture was being organized by Cardinal Pelagius–the ostensible spiritual (but virtual military) leader of the failed Fifth Crusade against al-Kamil at the siege of Damietta in

1219-1220. This new military campaign was now, however, to be aided by the mighty army of the Holy Roman Emperor Frederick II (who was long overdue to make good on his vow to go on crusade).[64] Agreement on the new enterprise was announced in April, 1223 at Ferentino; the date of departure was set for June, 1225. However, already by July, 1224, having overcome a series of daunting obstacles,[65] it was common knowledge that Frederick's complex preparations were nearing their completion and that he was making final arrangements in order to depart on time. To that end, papal envoys were dispatched to the imperial Diet at Nürnberg during the same month of July to discuss any possible last minute complications.[66]

Given this news, I am convinced that Francis went with a few of his closest companions to the hermitage of La Verna profoundly discouraged, perhaps even depressed, over the events about to unfold.[67] Once again, unable or unwilling to resolve human problems peacefully and fraternally through dialogue and mutual respect, the leaders of the Christian world were mobilizing their military might to engage in actions which

---

[64]Thomas C. Van Cleve, "The Crusade of Frederick II," *A History of the Crusades, II: The Later Crusades, 1189-1311* (Madison, Wisconsin: University of Wisconsin Press, 1969), 438-44, passim; see also Thomas C. Van Cleve, *The Emperor Frederick II of Hohenstaufen:* Immutator Mundi (Oxford: Clarendon Press, 1972), 158-61.

[65]Enthusiasm for the new venture was lacking in France and England (at war with each other) as well as in Spain (engaged in armed struggle with the Muslims) and even in Germany itself.

[66]Van Cleve, *Frederick II*, 161, note 1. The death of Frederick's wife, Constance, the previous year had, however, now opened up a tantalizing new possibility for the Emperor: marriage to Yolande of Brienne, heir to the throne of the Latin Kingdom of Jerusalem, would give him the crown as King of Jerusalem. The ceremony was performed in Brindisi only on November 9, 1225. By then, however, the date of departure had already been postponed indefinitely.

[67]I find it extremely significant that one of these chosen companions was Illuminato: the friar who had accompanied Francis into the camp of the Sultan at Damietta and who seems to be the sole conduit for an intimate knowledge of both of these experiences–Damietta and La Verna–for Bonaventure.

would inexorably lead to yet more bloodshed and death. More personally still, Francis stood in danger of seeing the death of a man he had come to view as an *amicus* and, even more importantly, as his *frater*:[68] someone he had come to know and apparently respect during that famous encounter with him under the tent in Damietta.[69] And so he goes to La Verna to do a "Lent of St. Michael"–an intense prayer of fasting dedicated to St. Michael the Archangel, who, by tradition, has been regarded as the guardian in battle *par excellence*–on behalf of his Muslim brother, Malik al-Kamil. And in the midst of this prayer, Francis has a profound mystical experience resulting in the appearance in his body of the wounds of Christ. Once the intensity of this experience had subsided, we are told by Leo, he called for some parchment and wrote the *Praises of God* on its front side. These *Praises*, it seems to me, laid out in simple staccato rhythm, are Francis's personalized version of *The Ninety-Nine Beautiful Names of Allah*.[70] In other words, Francis is praying in an Islamic mode:

---

[68] I will explain the somewhat unexpected use of these two terms in my conclusion.

[69] The encounter of Francis with the Sultan, Malik al-Kamil, has been extensively treated in recent years. The primary accounts are: Giulio Basetti-Sani, *Mohammed et Saint François* (Ottawa: Commissariat de Terre-Sainte, 1959); Giulio Basetti-Sani, *Per un dialogo cristiano-musulmano: Mohammed, Damietta et La Verna* (Milan: Vita e Pensiero, 1969); Gwénolé Jeusset, *Dieu est courtoisie: François d'Assise, son Ordre et l'Islam* (Rennes: n.p., 1985); idem, *Rencontre sur l'autre rive: François d'Assise et les Musulmans* (Paris: Éditions franciscaines, 1996); Jan Hoeberichts, *Francis and Islam* (Quincy, Illinois: Franciscan Press, 1997); Pauli Annala, "Frate Francesco e la quinta crociata," *Frate Francesco*, ns. 69 (2003): 409-25; and most recently Kathleen A. Warren, *Daring to Cross the Threshold: Francis of Assisi Encounters Sultan Malek al-Kamil* (Rochester, Minnesota: Sisters of St. Francis, 2003). John V. Tolan, a recognized expert in Muslim-Christian relations in the medieval world, is currently at work on a new scholarly examination of this encounter. I will return to the importance of this event in the last part of the article.

[70] *Ninety-nine Names of Allah: the Beautiful Names*, trans. Shems Friedlander and al-Hajj Shaikh Muzaffereddin (New York: Harper & Row, 1978); or Gazzali, *The Ninety-nine Beautiful Names of God = al-Maqsad al-asna: fi sharh asma' Allah al-husna*, trans. David B. Burrel and Nazih Daher (Cambridge:

You are love, charity; you are wisdom . . .
You are security, you are calm, you are joy;
You are our hope and gladness, you are justice . . .
You are protector, you are our guardian and defender . . .
You are strength, you are refreshment;
You are our hope, you are our faith, you are our charity . . .
You are our eternal life . . .[71]

Francis is praying in this manner precisely because the Sultan, Malik al-Kamil, is very much on his mind, weighing on his heart and troubling his spirit. Thus, what is usually interpreted as generic praise can now be seen in a different and more revealing light: namely, that Francis's praise to God for this mysterious gift of the stigmata is in a style of prayer which had moved and impressed him while in Egypt precisely because the events of those days and his affection for the Sultan were now present to him in an unmistakably poignant way.

And then, according to Leo, Francis turned the parchment over and wrote a prayer of protection for his friend–not for Leo but for Malik al-Kamil–asking:

May the Lord bless and guard you;
May the Lord show his face to you and be merciful to you;
May the Lord turn his face to you and give you peace.[72]

Cambridge University Press, 1992). Cf. Giulio Basetti-Sani, *La cristofania della Verna e le stigmate di san Francesco per il mondo musulmano*, Testimoni di un'Europa senza frontiere, 3 (San Pietro in Cariano: Il Segno, 1993), 139-42.

[71] LaudDei (Esser, 142): "*Tu es fortis, tu es magnus, tu es altissimus, tu es rex omnipotens. . . . Tu es amor, caritas; tu es sapientia, tu es humilitas, tu es patientia, tu es pulchritudo, tu es mansuetudo; tu es securitas; tu es quietas, tu es gaudium, tu es spes nostra et laetitia, tu es iustitia . . . tu es protector, tu es custos et defensor noster; tu es fortitudo, tu es refrigerium. Tu es nostra spes, tu es fides nostra, tu es caritas nostra, tu es tota dulcedo nostra, tu es vita aeterna nostra: Magnus et admirabilis Dominus, Deus omnipotens, misericors Salvator.*

[72] BenLeo (Esser, p. 143) and above, n. 46.

The word "guard" is indeed a more accurate translation of the word *"custodiat"* because we now know that al-Kamil's life was soon to be in danger.[73] In short, these familiar words of Aaron drawn from the Book of Numbers represent a blessing not for Brother Leo but for the Sultan.

But there is more. Francis then draws a head near the bottom of the parchment, complete with a makeshift turban and the stubble of a beard, placing the head in a recumbent position. He could have drawn the head upright, so as to be facing the one looking at the *chartula* and then, consistent both with the prayer of protection above and the use of the Tau as a talisman of protection as in the prophet Ezekiel, signed the *forehead* of the Sultan with this Tau. But Francis does not choose this construction. Rather, he positions the head on the ground, as it were, and has the Sultan actually confessing the Tau; for the Tau is actually emerging from his ***mouth*** (and not the forehead). Why this curious choice? Is he saying that the Sultan already confesses the cross of Christ (and the values which flow from such a confession),[74] or is he saying that he ought to, ***needs to***, proclaim the Christ before it is too late?

---

[73] BenLeo: *"Benedicat tibi Dominus et **custodiat** te. . . ."* It is important to stress that the Latin word here is *custodiat*: not "keep" (as the traditional rendering in English would have it) but "guard," or, better still, "guard from," especially from evil or harm. The verb *custodire* is extraordinarily important in the Franciscan lexicon. It is used by Francis to describe the specific function assigned to those who have been entrusted with a spiritual office–the *custos*–and whose role is to guard the friars entrusted to them from harm to their spiritual lives. Cf. the references, for example, in the *Regula pro eremitoriis* and the *Testament*. I explore these concepts and their related texts in an unpublished article: "Guardians and the Use of Authority among the Early Franciscans."

[74] One wonders whether this possible interpretation of the enigmatic figure–it is not the only one, as we will see–might be the origin of the account in the *Actus beati Francisci* where the Sultan and several members of his court are said to want to secretly be converted to Christianity but refrain from doing so due to the belief that they (as well as the two friars) would have been put to death. Instead, the account avers that the Sultan was baptized on his deathbed. Cf. *Actus* XXVII, 314-22. The account in the LMaj IX:8 simply has Francis himself asking the Sultan to be converted, without a positive outcome.

I think the latter reading is the more likely one. Indeed, I find it intriguing that in the High Middle Ages there existed a popular theme in vernacular literature of a person who, having died and seen the horrors of hell, returns to the earth as a head (or skull), confesses his errors in this life, and then urges others to a conversion of life–a conversion to Christ–before it is too late.[75] Moreover, in this same current of medieval literature, the person who comes back to confess his faith in Christ–or who speaks from a position between life and death–and urges others to do the same is very often portrayed as a non-believer, a Muslim, and indeed even a Muslim leader (a Sultan?).[76] It is

---

[75] This theme of different kinds of *"crânes mystérieux"* has recently been treated in a completely different context than the one studied here in a magisterial article: Claudio Galdersi, "Le 'crâne qui parle': du motif aux récits. Vertu chrétienne et vertu poétique," *Cahiers de Civilisation Médiévale* 46 (2003): 213-31. Although there are a number of different variations on the theme of these "talking heads," there are two distinct and diametrically opposed typologies. In the first, the skull is portrayed as living and then passes from life to death; in the second, the skull comes back from death to life in order to be reborn (in Christ) and then die a second (and harmless) death. It is the second typology (and its protype in the so-called legend of "Jesus and the Skull") that concerns us. In this line of stories, which dates from the 11th century forward, Jesus calls a person back to life in order to give that person the opportunity to confess one's faith in him. What is fascinating is that this line of the legend finds an echo in the Islamic world. Cf. the studies cited by Galdersi, for example: Fabrizio A. Pennacchietti, *Susanna nel deserto: riflessi di un racconto biblico nella cultura arabo-islamica* (Turin: Zamorani, 1998), 99-102; Fabrizio A. Pennacchietti "Le leggenda islamica del teschio redivivo in una versione neoaramaica," *Semitic and Cushitic Studies*, eds. Gideon Goldenberg and Shlomo Raz (Weisbaden: Harrassowitz, 1994), 103-32. The first Islamic reference to the legend of the damned raised up by Christ is found in "The Divine Book" (the *Elāhī-nāmé*) of the Sufi mystic Farid ad-Din (d. 1220). On this latter's use of the legend, see: F.A. Pennacchietti, "Il racconto di Giongiomé di Faridoddin Attàr e le sue fonti cristiane," *Orientalia Christiana Periodica* 62 (1996): 89-112 and Bianca Torta, *La leggenda islamica del teschio redivivo nelle fonti arabe*, Diss PhD., Università di Turin, 1994. Incidentally, note the resonance of the theme of *"la morte seconda"* in the second typology with the last refrain of the "Canticle of the Creatures," line 13.

[76] Cf. Galdersi (227-31) notes that this theme of the "talking skull" also found its way into the French vernacular version of the *Vitae patrum*, in at least two tales: *Vie des Pères*, II, no. xxv ("*Païen*") and III, no. lviii, ("*Crâne*"), ed. Félix

quite possible that Francis might have known of this popular legend and used it to depict his friend, Malik al-Kamil, as confessing the Christ (represented in the form of a Tau, the cross of Christ), as a prayer for him to do the same before it would be too late and he would be lost for all eternity. It was, in reality, the only thing he could do for his brother.

Finally, it seems that Francis would then have written a Latin word across the shaft of the Tau. Is this word, however, to be read as *fleo* or, using the shaft itself as the letter "T," as *fle(T)o* or even as *fle(T)ote*? This is the most difficult problem that has bedeviled interpreters of the *chartula*.

For if one assumes–as I am assuming here–that the blessing from the Book of Numbers was intended as a prayer of protection for the Sultan and not for Leo, then the so-called blessing for Brother Leo refers only to the words in section [4] of the verso side of the parchment: that is, *Dominus benedicat f le o te* (or, as some would read them, *Dominus benedicat f[rater] Leo te*). This is the standard reading accepted by most scholars. However, the words themselves are highly problematic for they are poor (that is to say, incorrect) Latin.[77] One might easily excuse Francis, the son of a merchant, for making such an error–except that he knew full well that the verb *benedicare* takes the dative (*tibi*) and not the accusative (*te*) because he had

---

Lecoy, Société des Anciens Textes Français (Paris: Picard, 1993, 1998), 49-60 and 210-16, esp. 213, respectively. Here, the legend represents a third typology that simply attests to the immutability of the truth proclaimed about salvation in Christ but also gives witness to the development of the imagery used within the legend. In "*Crâne*," the word of truth which attests to the necessity of believing in Christ that is addressed to Christians and non-Christians alike, is entrusted no longer to Christ but to the skull itself who is a pagan, a non-believer. This is taken a step further in "*Païen*" where the testimony is entrusted not just to a non-believer but a Saracen, indeed a Saracen leader (Sultan?). Indeed, it is the tears of a hermit ("the tears that resurrect") that awaken in the Muslim the desire to convert and confess the Christ (cf. "*Païen*," 50-51). Moreover, the Muslim is neither in paradise nor in hell but can see both the sufferings of the damned and the joy of the elect. The parallels between this particular tradition and what Francis depicts on the verso side of the *chartula* need to be explored further.

[77]Cf. Fleming, "Iconographic Unity," 206-07.

just written it above in the famous blessing of Aaron (*Dominus benedicat tibi*. . .). How then is one to make sense of the awkward and incorrect use of the word *"te"* in this blessing for Leo?[78]

The most convincing explanation, to my mind, would be to assume that the word or words through the shaft of the Tau were actually written first–for a purpose completely extraneous to Leo–and that the letters *"te"* belonged (at least initially) to the word written through the Tau and not to the so-called Blessing for Leo.

If credible, then what word did Francis write through the Tau after having finished his drawing of the Sultan? And does the Tau function as the letter "t" or not? Each possible word– *fleo*, *fle(T)o* and *fle(T)ote* – answers certain questions but poses other problems as well.

Given the various possibilities available to us and following the suggestion made by John V. Fleming, it seems possible that the most likely word Francis would have added to the drawing

---

[78]There are three possible explanations: (1) Francis composed a blessing for Leo, comprising all the words under and through the cross [4], and made a grammatical error (even though he had used the correct form in the Aaronic blessing); (2) Francis composed a blessing for Leo by attaching it to a word already written through the Tau, unable to resist the coincidence between the word *fle o* and *f(rater) Leo*, adding the personal pronoun *"te,"* knowing it was bad Latin; or (3) Francis composed a blessing for Leo by attaching it to a word already written through the Tau, unable to resist the coincidence between the letters *fle o te* and *f(rater) Leo te*, knowing the words were not really correct Latin but close enough to compose a clever blessing for his distressed friend. Given these three possible explanations, I would prefer the third explanation whereby the grammatical "error" would already have been present on the parchment (i.e., the *"te"* was not added by Francis) but accepted as such since it suited well enough his intended purpose: to give consolation to the troubled friar. This explanation is reinforced, it seems, by the fact that Francis was insistent on wedging such a blessing under the right arm of the Tau and attaching it to the word intersecting the Tau cross. Indeed, he could have more easily written such a blessing right underneath the Aaronic blessing since at that time there was still ample room for such a phrase in that space. The fact that he chose not to leads one to believe that another dynamic was operative–the existence of a word already on the page.

was *fle(T)ote*–"You must (soon) weep!" or "May you (soon) weep!"–using the Tau cross as a functional "t" in the word written.[79] Although the word *fle(T)ote* conveniently explains the awkwardness of the "*te*" appended onto *f(rater) Le o*, it also, however, raises a critical question: would Francis have known the plural form of the verb *flere* in this obscure formulation of the future imperative?[80] And if he did, then whom is he addressing with this call to weep sometime in the near future and in what context? One could make a convincing case that the future plural form of the verb *flere* might be an exasperated plea to Christian leaders in the West to weep over the nefarious venture they are about to undertake in Egypt against Islam and the Sultan Malik al-Kamil.

But one can make an equally convincing argument in favor of the view that the word through the Tau is the more simple word *fleo* with the ungrammatical "*te*" supplied in reference to the Sultan. In this scenario, Francis himself would be weeping for the Sultan, praying that he confess the Christ before it was too late.

---

[79]But there are two other possibilities. The word *fle(t)o* could be either the singular 2nd or 3rd person of the same verb *flere* also in its future imperative formulation. But again–whom is he addressing in a future moment: the Sultan or someone else? But then, in this instance, the "*te*" must be considered part of the appended blessing to Leo, as an incorrect and inexcusable use of the accusative. In the third possibility, the simple word *fleo* (without incorporating the use of the Tau) would be a simple indicative statement: "I weep" or even with the added but incorrect "*te*," "I am weeping *for you*." One could make a persuasive case that Francis would be saying or, in fact, praying that his tears on behalf of al-Kamil would release the mercy of the Lord and prompt the conversion and confession of the Sultan, just like in the vernacular version of the popular legend. This is, in some respects, the most attractive option, except for its incorrect use of the word "*te*" since all five elements–the Aaronic blessing, the Tau, the head, the writing and the crude map of the sea–would then relate directly to al-Kamil himself. One would have to allow Francis to have made a grammatical error on an obscure word–not an implausible concession–and, just as it is in the appended blessing to Leo, not have the Tau serve as the letter "t."

[80]Other aspects of the Fleming thesis–like his contention that Francis was constructing a clever acrostic–appear more questionable to me.

In both hypotheses, Francis's use of this unusual verb is part of his prayer on behalf of the Sultan begun already with the blessing from Numbers. In the first, it would represent an anguished call to conversion–a conversion of life, attitudes and actions–for those who would continue on the path to bloodshed rather than the path to peace and reconciliation. In the second, it would represent a more direct prayer for the Sultan himself and a tearful concern for his impending fate.

Whichever scenario is the more likely, it is at this point–after Francis had completed his prayer for the Sultan–that Brother Leo would have come to him with his personal crisis. As his friend and father, Francis would have added the famous words which, when appended onto the existing call to weep, would have awkwardly constituted a kind of blessing for the forlorn brother.[81] Francis would then have given Leo the tiny parchment for his consolation and safe-keeping, maintaining silence on its *allocutio*–its secret message–so intimate had been the experience of the stigmatization vision and the fruit of that mystical encounter now put to parchment.

Conclusion

If this reconstruction of events and analysis of the texts are fairly accurate, then we can make the following final observations.

In 1219 Francis had gathered the friars in Chapter and told them that he and several companions were going to Egypt in

---

[81] Nothing in this interpretation, incidentally, contradicts what Leo tells us in his third explication [3]: *"Beatus Franciscus scripsit manu sua istam benedictionem mihi fratri Leoni."* Although the reader typically assumes that Leo is referring to the blessing above as well as below, there is nothing whatsoever in his words that impedes us from believing that he may be referring only to the little blessing appended below it or that he mistakenly assumed that Francis had intended both for him. It is the awkwardness of the placement of the little blessing and the infelicitous use (or acceptance) of the Latin that causes one to wonder whether more is going on here than, perhaps, Leo himself actually knew.

the company of a contingent of the Fifth Crusade. When asked why he was going to a place where he might lose his life, he told them–in what is sometimes called his *Testament of 1219*– that those who were commonly considered their enemies (*inimici*), those whom Christian society and especially the Church have told them insistently were the sworn enemies of Christ, the infidel *par excellence*, who could hand them over to punishment and even death: such people, the Muslims in Egypt, were in fact their *amici* (their friends).[82] But if Francis considered the Muslims *amici*, it was not in the sense that they were emotionally friendly to each other, had a personal bond as friends, but, more profoundly, that he considered them to be–knew them to be–his *fratres* (his brothers). Francis told his friars that he was going to Egypt not only to preach this message but to manifest it in his own life and actions, even if it might cost him his life. This was the vision he had dedicated his whole life to living.

This profound statement was but the logical and bold extension, the implication as it were, of what had been so indelibly revealed to him at the moment of his conversion in 1206. Led among the lepers outside Assisi, Francis had come to the cardinal insight of his life: namely, that all men and women without exception were creatures of the same Creator God; that all men and women were endowed with the same dignity and

---

[82] RNB 23: 1-4: "Let all the brothers attend to what the Lord says: *Love your enemies and do good to those who hate you* (Mt 5: 44). For even the Lord Jesus Christ, whose footsteps we follow (cf. 1 Peter 2: 21), called his betrayer **"friend"** and freely gave himself up to those who crucified him. They are our **friends**, therefore, all those who unjustly inflict on us trials, anxieties, shame and injuries, suffering and torture, martyrdom and death. We should love them greatly, for out of what they inflict on us we have eternal life." It is David Flood who has originated the term "Testament of 1219" to describe this text. However, whereas he believes the entire chapter constitutes the farewell address, it is my contention that only the first four verses ought to be considered part of such a message. The rest seems more consistent with what might be the core of the resignation sermon given by Francis to his friars in September, 1220. Cf. David Flood and Thaddée Matura, *The Birth of a Movement* (Chicago: Franciscan Herald Press, 1975), 95.

worth and received the same grace of salvation; that all, without exception, were *fratres et sorores*, brothers and sisters one to another. This is, what I have called elsewhere, Francis's insight of the universal fraternity of all creatures, especially those most difficult of creatures: human beings. Therefore, everything that breaks the bonds of this sacred human fraternity created by God–through violence and bloodshed, through the destructive and abusive use of power, through the placing of oneself over and against others for the private advantage of one to the disadvantage of others–is what, for Francis, constitutes sin. Moreover, to understand what Francis means by sin is to understand what he means when he says that he began to "do penance." "To do penance" is to distance oneself from all those actions and attitudes that threaten to rupture the bonds of the human fraternity. And to understand what he means by penance is to understand the essential content of the penitential preaching of Francis and his brothers.[83]

This message–this vision–of the universal fraternity of all creatures is what Francis and his brothers went to the Holy Land in 1219 to live out and to share. This background–which escapes the notice of most crusade historians–has profound ramifications for understanding the succeeding events in Francis's life. For Francis went to Egypt 1219 to oppose the continued bloodshed of the Fifth Crusade.[84] He first attempted to turn the crusaders from their intended assault on the camp of

---

[83]I recapitulate here a central argument both of my treatment of Francis of Assisi in my dissertation (*La renonciation au pouvoir chez les Frères*, chapter 1, pages 34-39) and encapsulated in my article "Hermitage or Marketplace: The Search for an Authentic Franciscan *locus* in the World (Revised Version)," *True Followers of Justice: Identity, Insertion and Itinerancy among the Early Franciscans*, Spirit and Life 10 (St. Bonaventure, New York: The Franciscan Institute, 2000), 1-30, esp. 10-14.

[84]On Francis's opposition to the Fifth Crusade, see the excellent article of James Powell, "Francesco d'Assisi e la Quinta Crociata," *Schede Medievali* 4 (1983): 68-77. The article is a brilliant exposition of the account of Francis's presence and actions at Damietta found in 2 Celano 30, the most important account about the event.

the Sultan Malik al-Kamil at Damietta. The soldiers' response: they mocked him. And they were roundly defeated. Then, during the ensuing weeks, he and a companion, Brother Illuminato, went across enemy lines into the camp of the Muslims. And after some initial problems, they entered into a respectful dialogue with the Sultan and his spiritual counselors. Risking danger and possibly even death, he and his companion lived out their vision of the universal fraternity of all creatures, reaching out in dialogue to the one considered most inimical to it. The three then parted amicably–a profound exchange having occurred and a lasting bond having been established.

In early August 1224, accompanied by several companions, Francis would have gone to La Verna with a deeply aggrieved spirit but with the intention of doing a "Lent of St. Michael" in supplication to God concerning the deteriorating situation between Christianity and Islam, and was his fervent prayer for the protection of his friend, Malik al-Kamil. And it does not seem insignificant that he went there in the company of Illuminato, his companion in Damietta.[85] It is probably no exaggeration to posit that Francis would have gone there disturbed and even confused about the values that had been revealed to him by God through his encounter with the lepers: values which had consistently shaped the contours of his whole life; values which had inexorably led him to adopt a posture of radical non-violence in relationship to the human community, so much in need of further healing and not further destruction. And yet the Church of his day, backed by immense military force, insisted on another way, impelled by different set of values.

In the course of this intense period of fasting, on or around the Feast of the Exaltation of the Cross, inwardly tormented,

---

[85]Illuminato knew the importance of those events in Damietta and with the Sultan and may have been the one–the only one–who kept alive the meaning of those events for Francis in his conversations with Bonaventure in preparation for the *Legenda maior*.

Francis entered into a profound meditation upon the mystery of the passion of Jesus Christ or, more precisely, the image of Christ lifted up on the cross as a sign of healing for the human race, drawn from the Gospel of John 3 (or John 12). This meditation became transformed into mystical ecstasy in which he himself experienced– as the author of the *Fioretti* puts it–the love which Christ felt for humanity in giving himself on the cross and the pain that was an integral part of that act of ultimate self-giving.[86] The fruit of this intense prayer manifested itself in Francis becoming, as it were, the very object of his prayer: a crucified man marked with the stigmata.

But why did the image of Christ on the cross have such resonance within Francis to the extent that it would transport him into so intimate an experience of ecstasy and result in him tasting such incredible sweetness and abiding solace?

The reason can be found in what the cross of Jesus Christ had come to symbolize and mean for Francis. For in his later writings, Francis had developed what can only be called a veritable mysticism of the cross in which the cross of Christ had become for him the quintessential sign of the non-violent response of Jesus of Nazareth to the violence and injustices of the world.[87] He who opened his arms on the cross, refusing to respond to the violence done to him with a reciprocal act of violence, accepting out of love for the human race even death, has, through that very act (the Gospel of John tells us), brought healing and salvation to the world. In so doing, the cross of Christ has become the sign of full and true obedience to the Father's will: not in the mechanical and masochistic sense of certain medieval and contemporary soteriologies; but obedience

---

[86] *I Fioretti*, 226.

[87] The three most critical texts are: the Letter to the Minister, the Salutation to the Virtues and the Testament. Cf. my dissertation, *La renonciation au pouvoir*, 104-22, but especially the previously mentioned unpublished article: "Guardians and the Use of Authority among the Early Franciscans" where I treat more systematically and in greater depth the theme of the cross in these texts.

in the sense of a total commitment to what God wants for the human race and how God wants us to live with each other in the human fraternity he has created us to be and wills us to be (if only we would live like his Son). But these actions will bring one inevitably into conflict with the ways of the world, with the carnal spirit, with evil cloaked by power as virtue–with all the consequences of such a clash. This is the way of the cross and the way of the gospel; it is, therefore, the *forma vitae fratrum minorum*.

As such, the vision of the seraphic Christ lifted up on the cross for the healing of the world indelibly confirmed for Francis and in Francis what had been revealed to him during his encounter with the lepers: that all members of the human fraternity were sacred creatures of God and that every attitude and action that does violence to this sacred community must be repented of; that this vision was indeed true and trustworthy; that it was, in fact, salvific. Far from having wasted his life attempting to live out this radical vision, Francis found himself validated by God on La Verna as a truly evangelical man, an authentic obedient servant, faithful to the values of Jesus Christ, and him crucified.

If Christ upon the cross is the quintessential example of the non-violent Jesus, the cross of Christ is also what it means to be *minor et subditus omnibus* (minor and subject to all): that bedrock posture of Francis and his movement which is found articulated throughout the *opuscula* from the first layers of the Early Rule; to his instruction on the manner of exercising authority among the brothers; to the behavior of those friars sent on mission among the Saracens; to the heart-rending advice given to the aggrieved minister in the Letter to a Minister; to the final lines of the Salutation of the Virtues where true obedience is once again compared to the non-violent Jesus on the cross, refusing to reply in violence to violence and injustice, even to the point of death on a cross. And yet, paradoxically and scandalously, only in such a way will the human heart and the world be healed.

The seraphic vision, therefore, confirmed Francis in his deepest existential and spiritual convictions. It filled him with great and abiding solace and at the same time generated within him ecstatic praise to God for having reconfirmed this in the depths of his soul, indeed in his very flesh. This is what led him to give praise to God in the simplest of terms, in the mode of his Islamic brothers and sisters and his newly discovered *frater*, for whom he had been praying. For even in death, if one is faithful to the values of love manifested by and incarnated in the Crucified One, his meditation now assured him, will the healing of the human race be achieved.

La Verna thus joins Damietta to Assisi; and Assisi to all who would live the evangelical life of peace and reconciliation. But even more: La Verna turns one of the greatest Christian mythic images on its very head. For contrary to the story of the sign given to Constantine in the clouds above, assuring him of military victory over his enemies through the sword and resulting in the ultimate advance of Christianity in the western world, Francis was given a vastly different sign–a sign not of violence but of love unto death–lifted up above him for the healing of the world (East and West), indeed all of human history. For only *in hoc signo vinces*–only in **this** sign–Francis was assured on La Verna, will you ever truly conquer.

The *Camoscio*:
Relic of the Side Wound of Francis of Assisi, "Living Eucharist"[1]

Carla Salvati

Reach out your hand and put it in my side.
Do not doubt but believe (John 20:27).

According to Thomas of Celano, when Francis of Assisi discovered relics in an abandoned church "he commanded the brothers to move with all reverence the holy relics . . . to the place of the brothers. He felt very bad that they had been robbed of the devotion due them for a long time."[2] Francis's own relics–habits, shoes and other objects–have been carefully preserved by his Order. Perhaps the most mysterious are the relics of the stigmata: the habit Francis wore on Mount La Verna, bloodstained bandages and shoes, even tiny ampules of blood believed to have issued from the wounds. But, while scholarship has been intensely focused on textual and iconographic sources for the cult of the stigmata, no study to date has given due attention to the relics. These physical traces provide a unique vantage point from which to examine the reception of the miracle of Mount La Verna where, according to the pervading belief, mystical union with Christ occurred as much in the flesh as in the spirit.

The most visually dramatic and symbolically rich of all the relics of the stigmata of St. Francis of Assisi is the one known as the *camoscio*, a leather bandage which Francis wore to protect his side wound from the coarseness of his habit. The relic, part of the collection of the Basilica of St. Francis in Assisi, is in a solar-shaped monstrance.[3] (See fig. 1, next page). At first sight the *camoscio* appears damaged, the center torn. The portion that would have made contact with the side wound, the most sacred part of the relic, is missing. But the longer we look, the more the tear at its center emerges as the "content" framed by the reliquary. The Eucharistic monstrance seems to be offering the *camoscio*

Figure 1

not merely as a contact relic of the side wound of Francis, but as the bearer of the actual size and shape of the wound. The impact is powerful, drawing the viewer in, demanding a response. Through the poetics of imagery, the absence [of material] at the center of the *camoscio* becomes the presence of the side wound; the side wound (consecrated by the Eucharistic monstrance) is translated into a miraculous host, and Francis's stigmatized body is transformed into a living Eucharist. (See opposite page.)

The presentation of the relic effectively draws together theological beliefs and perceptions of the meaning of St. Francis's stigmatization current from the 13th through the 17th centuries. That this is not a question of unconscious artistry can be seen by viewing the *camoscio* and its Eucharistic framing in the light of the medieval devotion to the measurement of the side wound of Christ (the *mensura vulneris*), the Eucharistic symbolism of the side wound, and a sermon delivered in Rome in 1672 by the Jesuit Antonio Vieira, who compares stigmatization with transubstantiation.

To begin with, the *camoscio*, along with the other relics associated with the care of the stigmata, has an intimate connection to the medieval devotion to the wounds of Christ. For the first ten centuries of its history, Christian piety was not especially focused on the wounds. They were essentially used as a proof in the polemics surrounding the Resurrection and Christ's human/divine nature. A real devotion to the Five Wounds belongs to the medieval period and its intense focus on Christ's humanity and the Passion. From the thirteenth century onwards, devotion to "woundedness," which may well have resonated with the difficult lives of medieval believers, found expression in practices accessible to all.[4] Books of Hours were full of prayers to the Five Wounds. The devout could attend the Mass of the Five Wounds or celebrate the Feast of the Five Wounds. Devotion could be expressed by gestures as simple as genuflecting five times or as onerous as fasting for five days.[5]

The stigmatization of St. Francis acted as a powerful catalyst for these devotions. According to Louis Gougaud, "The triumphal event of the five wounds in the veneration of the Middle Ages truely dates from the stigmatization of LaVerna, "the great miracle . . ."[6] Just as St. Bernard made devotion to the Passion part of the life of a monk, the preaching of the Franciscans, charged with enthusiasm for the stigmata, spread the devotion for the Passion and the Five Wounds beyond the cloister and into the daily lives of believers. And, while Francis's wounds were often depicted as iconic, Christ-like and miraculous, the relics of the stigmata were not simply seen as evidence of an abstract or metaphoric woundedness. They spoke of real human suffering.

Though the early sources do not mention the *camoscio* specifically, they do make reference to pieces of cloth (*pezze*) placed over the stigmata by Brother Leo to stop the bleeding. The following is from the *Actus Beati Francisci et Sociorum Eius*, Consideration 3:

> And although those very holy wounds, inasmuch as they were imprinted on him by Christ, gave him very great joy in his heart, nevertheless they gave unbearable pain to his flesh and physical senses. . . .[F]orced by necessity, he chose Br. Leo . . . and entrusted his wounds only to him to be touched and rebound with new bandages.[7]

Dressings would stick, causing him "pain . . . from the loosening of the bloody bandages."[8] This passage reveals Francis's daily experience, the "unbearable pain" he felt, his vulnerability and need of Brother Leo's help. Here there is no questioning of the reality of the stigmata; these are real wounds, requiring the same care and causing the same pain as any ordinary wound.[9] Yet they are not ordinary wounds, they are "holy wounds" and the bandages were not discarded as ordinary bandages would have been; they were preserved by the friars and are found listed in Inventory Catalogues as the *pezze* "the pieces of cloth with which he [Brother Leo] dried his wounds."[10]

While the *pezze* were used for all the wounds, the *impiastro* is a relic particular to the care of the side wound, still carefully preserved by Clare's Sisters in the Monastery of St. Clare in Assisi. It is the most ephemeral of the relics of the stigmata, all that remain are shreds of stained linen housed in a silver casket.[11] (See fig. 2, opposite page.)

An *impiastro* is a poultice or herbal dressing made by spreading a paste of medicinal herbs on a linen cloth. According to Franciscan tradition, Clare prepared such herbal dressings and sent them to Francis to place on the *camoscio* before applying it to the side wound.

The earliest known mention of the *impiastro* is in the fourteenth-century *De Conformitate* of Bartholomew of Pisa, "Blessed Clare saw the stigmata of St. Francis while he was still alive and made an *impiastro* for the side wound which today can be seen in the Monastery of St. Clare in Assisi."[12] In the *Annales Minorum* Luke Wadding reports that he saw the *impiastro* in Assisi, but in his description he uses *impiastro* and *camoscio* interchangeably:

> In the church of St. George of the Poor Clares in Assisi I saw preserved a kind of cataplasm or poultice (*impiastro*) (in old vernacular Italian, *camocium*), which the most Holy Virgin Clare made for the holy man to soothe the pain of the wound and to stop the bleeding.[13]

The herbal balm prepared by Clare "to soothe the pain of the wound" exposes not only the daily pain Francis endured but Clare's pain in seeing him suffer. In an age associated with a harsh asceticism inspired by the wounds inflicted on Christ by humanity, the *impiastro*

Figure 2

tells of Clare's attempts to soothe the pain and heal the wound inflicted on Francis by Christ himself. If Christ in his divine nature is understood to have carved the wounds out of Francis's flesh, his human nature seems to be reflected in Francis's pain and Clare's compassion.

Like the *pezze* and the *impiastro*, the *camoscio* directs our attention to the fact that Francis's wounds were open, bleeding and required daily care, but the tear at its centre also introduces an element of mystery. To my knowledge, the earliest description of the *camoscio* is in the Liturgical Catalogue of Relics of the Basilica of St. Francis in Assisi (ca. 1338).[14] The Catalogue was used for the yearly blessing with the relics: as the priest raised each relic to perform the blessing, its description was read aloud to the congregation.[15] The reading for the *camoscio* was *Item est unum corium perfusum sanguine, cum quo cooperiebat vulnus lateralis, et viditur esse lanceatum* (Here is a piece of leather, soaked with blood, which covered the side wound and it appears as if pierced with a lance).[16]

We know therefore that the *camoscio* had its lance-shaped tear as early as the fourteenth century. Perhaps, as Bonaventure Mariangeli suggests, the missing piece was cut out because it was soaked with blood and is the item referred to as the blood relics of Francis listed in the Inventories of the Basilica in Assisi.[17] It is unlikely however that the shape of the tear was accidental since its description, "as if pierced with a lance," corresponds exactly to the description of Francis's side wound found in thireteenth-century sources. In the encyclical letter which first announced the stigmata to the world, Brother Elias writes, "His side appeared pierced with a lance (*lanceatum apparuit*) and it often oozed blood."[18] And his contemporary Thomas of Celano uses the same words: "His right side was marked with an oblong red scar as if pierced by a lance."[19] It is clear that the description of the *camoscio*, "as if pierced with a lance," was meant to invoke the shape of Francis's wound, as though the contact relic had somehow become marked with the outline of the wound it had pressed against.

A seventeenth-century guide to Assisi includes a description of the *camoscio* which also mentions the *impiastro*:

> [A] piece of chamois medicated by St. Clare, which Francis wore on the sacred side wound, with the blood, the herbal dressing and the imprint of the wound, is carried in solemn procession through the streets of the city. . . .[20]

The author of the guide suggests that traces of blood and the poultice made by Clare were visible on the *camoscio*. More important, he draws the pilgrims' attention to the tear and informs them it is an imprint of the side wound.

These reiterations, the almost insistent implication that the side wound had miraculously transferred its size and shape to the bandage meant to bind and soothe it, are suggestive of the widespread 14th and 15th century practice of devotion to the *mensura vulneris*, the measurement of the side wound of Christ. Life-sized images of the side wound appeared on woodcut prints and in Books of Hours; images of the wounds, particularly the side wound, were carried for protection as amulets. The devotion was part of a medieval fascination with the precise length and breadth of *praesentia*. The measurements of Christ and the Virgin, the Holy Sepulchre and the Cross were all preserved as treasures in relic collections and listed in relic inventories. Holy pictures and prayer scrolls with the measurements of Christ were carried by the devout for protection.[21] Especially popular was the measurement of the side wound, usually estimated as 7 cm.[22] One example is from a fifteenth-century Book of Hours in which the wound is presented diagonally framed by a lozenge-shaped enclosure (see fig. 3 below).[23]

The images of this measurement were not seen as symbols of the side wound, but as relics, remnants of the wound, the exact outline of its *praesentia*. This is clearly illustrated in a Parisian Book of Hours, ca. 1485-1500 in which an image of the side wound of Christ is in a reliquary, carried by two angels.[24] (See fig. 4, below.)

According to Gougaud, "It also happens that this form might be indicated on the *estampes* through a simple slice in the paper."[25] This is what the devotee was meant to see in the *camoscio* relic, a cut out of the wound, an outline of the

Figure 3

Figure 4

"tear" in Francis's flesh.[26] But the tear in the *camoscio* was not merely a cut out of paper or wood made by a human hand, it was seen as the work of the wound itself; and mounted in the Eucharistic monstrance the piece of chamois looks as though it were Francis's own skin stretched onto the round frame, pulled tight to expose the "tear" in the center, the opening of the wound (see fig. 5, opposite page). It exposes the most venerable of the wounds inflicted on Mount La Verna, when Christ "tore the sack of flesh in that five-fold way."[27]

Bonaventure tells us that, though Francis tried to hide the side wound during his lifetime, some friars devised ways to catch a glimpse of it: "One brother . . . induced him with a pious care to take off his tunic to shake it out . . . [H]e saw the wound, and he even quickly touched it with three of his fingers determining the size of the wound by both sight and touch.[28] The *camoscio* exposes what the friar went to lengths to discover, the exact shape and size of the wound.

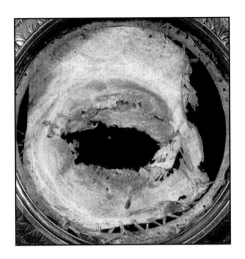

Figure 5

The initial descriptions of Francis's side as "as if pierced by a lance," the fact that, from its first mention in 1338, descriptions of the *camoscio* almost always note its lance-like tear, and the fascination with the size and shape of the wound are telling. There is an unmistakable echo of John 19:34 (". . . one of the soldiers pierced his side with a spear") which makes the side wound of Francis resonate with that of Christ. And the tear in the *camoscio*, the absence which is the visible evidence, evokes the wounds of both Francis and Christ. The relationship is intensified and brought to a new echelon by the framing of the relic in the Eucharistic monstrance.

The silver solar-shaped monstrance dates from 1602 and was commissioned by Father Cornelius Rosa, whose emblem is engraved on the pedestal.[29] First introduced in the 1400s, solar-shaped ostensories represented a trend away from monstrances in the form of a cross or statue of Christ, with the host sometimes exposed behind glass, over the side wound.[30] According to Timothy Verdon, by the mid-fifteenth century most Eucharistic monstrances were shaped like the sun, symbol of Christ, "The true light, which enlightens everyone" (John 1:9). Verdon suggests they may have been modeled on the rays that surround the holy name of Jesus, *IHS*, on the tablet of St. Bernardine of Siena[31] (see fig. 6). The Eucharistic monstrance that frames the *camoscio* has the same straight and undulating rays of St. Bernardine's tablet. It presents the *camoscio* ablaze with Seraphic fire.

While the *camoscio*, like the *impiastro*, is associated with the care of the side wound, in

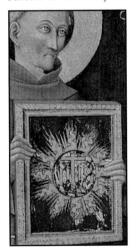

Figure 6

its Eucharistic frame its meaning becomes interwoven with the complex theology and symbolism of the side wound of Christ, source of the Eucharist. Its presentation in this way is not arbitrary, but rather takes its place in the history of an iconographic and hagiographic interpretation of Francis's relationship to Christ's wounds that culminates in Francis's assimilation into Christ.

On 13th and 14th century crucifixes, Francis draws the devotee's gaze to Christ's wounds. He is most often found next to the wounds, touching them, kissing them or gazing at them. On the *Crucifix of the Maestro della Santa Chiara* (ca. 1260) for instance, Francis is shown gazing into Christ's wound as though trying to penetrate its mystery. On a similar crucifix in the Basilica of San Francesco in Arezzo (ca.1270), Francis holds and kisses Christ's wounded foot in such a way that the blood flowing from the wound in his right hand appears indistinguishable from the blood of Christ.[32] A most explicit portrayal of Christ anointing Francis with his blood is captured on the *Crucifix with St Francis* (ca. 1315) by the Master of the San Quirico Cross, in which Francis is showered with the flow from the side wound of Christ.[33] (See figures 7 and 8, opposite page.)

In these images, Francis gazes, holds, touches and is touched by the wounds of Christ, and perhaps his tears–the grace of tears of which Bonaventure says, "such tears must be drawn from the Saviour's Fountains, i.e. from the five wounds"[34]–mingle with the blood of Christ. He is even anointed with and stigmatized by the blood of the wounds. Still, he remains outside the body of Christ, outside the mystery of the Passion.

But Francis is understood to have gone farther, and more than imitation of these examples of piety is required of the devotee. Just as the tear at the center of the 17th century Eucharistic framing of the *camoscio* draws the viewer in, so Bonaventure exhorts 13thcentury Franciscans not to merely gaze at or touch the wounds in Christ's hands, nor to simply reach into the side wound, but to enter bodily by the door in His side and go straight up to the very Heart of Jesus. There, burning with love for Christ Crucified, be transformed into Christ.[35]

In effect, [this is] to follow Francis on the path that he was believed to have taken metaphorically, literally, and mystically.

The initial step in Francis's penetration of the mystery of the Passion and assimilation into Christ through the side wound is the metaphoric underpinning of the story of his first visit to Mount La Verna. In the version of the Spanish friar Antonio Daza, in his treatise on the stigmata written in 1619, Francis went to La Verna in search of a secluded place to pray. Amongst the broken and split rocks he saw one so large and so seemingly suspended in air, supported only by a small stone, that he could not believe it to be the work of human hands:

> In the end the Saint entered into the cavity in the rock . . . begging the Lord to show him the reason for this great marvel . . . .When the Saint had finished praying, there appeared before him an Angel who said to him, "Francesco, this stone, just as many others which you see on this mountain split asunder on the death of our Lord Jesus Christ."[36]

In this story, Francis's desire to commune with Christ led him to Mount La Verna, the "mystic Calvary,"[37] a natural shrine of the Passion which had caused the earth to shake and rocks to split. The Passion for which, as Bonaventure put it, "heaven and earth mourn and hard rocks crack as if out of natural compassion."[38] On Mount La Verna, Francis is seen to have penetrated the "wounds" of the earth which had "mourned" the death of Christ, venturing further than anyone before him in penetrating the mystery of Calvary, something he could only have done by divine inspiration.

Figure 7

Figure 8

The belief in Francis's union with Christ, his assimilation into Christ's body after the stigmatization in 1224, again on La Verna, was sometimes expressed in stories in which he literally "inhabits" the side wound. A story from the thirteenth-century *Chronicle of Brother Thomas of Eccleston* and that of *Brother Jordan of Giano* tells of "heretics" who were scandalized to hear that the stigmata had exalted Francis above John the Evangelist. They had a vision in which they saw Jesus and John "reclining in the bosom" one of the other and took this as "confirmation of their opinion." But:

> ... lo, sweet Jesus with His own hands opened the wound in His side and there was seen most clearly Saint Francis within His breast, and sweet Jesus closed the wound, and shut him up entirely therein.[39]

By virtue of the stigmata, Francis's relation with Christ surpassed that of anyone who had preceded him; only Francis became "indistinguishable" from Christ; only his body was forever assimilated into Christ's, "shut up entirely" in his side wound.

The 15th century *La Franceschina* recounts a similar story, but with an added edge. It concerns a friar who continually prays Jesus to show him St. Francis. He has a vision in which procession after glorious procession passes by: first of confessors guiding St. Augustine and St. Gregory; then of "martyr saints, led by Saints Stephen and Laurence"; then of the Apostles; and then of the "Virgin Mother of God surrounded by holy virgins." Each time he asks if St. Francis is among them; each time the answer is "no" and the friar bids them go on. Finally come Christ and the angels, and again the friar asks after Francis. St. Michael gaily intercedes and Christ responds:

> "It pleases me; let the friar see him." And the Lord lifted his right arm and as he lifted it St. Francis emerged from the side wound of Our Lord Jesus Christ. On seeing St. Francis the friar's heart was filled with joy and consolation and he ran to him, at which point St. Francis cried out, "O you little wicked one, what are you doing? This is the Lord Jesus Christ before you." And the friar ... threw himself at the Lord's feet, recognizing his error.[40]

In his great enthusiasm to see Francis, the friar overlooks Christ and though he finally recognizes his error, it is too late, the damage is done. The narrative reverses the usual relationship between Christ and his saint, placing Christ in the role of mediator, revealing Francis hidden away in his side wound. Though Francis is outraged by the zealous friar's great oversight, Christ is complicit with the story's surprise ending: he is the one who granted Francis this most privileged place in the procession of saints, a place even more privileged than the Virgin's.

The idea of Francis resident in Christ had enough currency to be used in polemics against the Franciscans. An example of this is an illustration in a French edition of the antagonistic *Alcoran* which mockingly shows Francis, often called Christ's standard-bearer, waving his flag as he pokes out of the side wound.[41] (See fig. 9, below.)

Depictions of Francis physically emerging from Christ in such a concrete, almost prosaic way were literal interpretations of what was more profoundly seen as a mystical conflation of Christ and Francis. They are manifestations of the belief that after the stigmatization, Francis's followers had only to point to Christ, in particular to the wound in his side, to indicate Francis. The pivotal point is that Francis was placed in the side wound. This was the most venerated of Christ's wounds, considered to be the source of the sacraments: the water and blood that issued from Christ's side symbolized the water of Baptism and the blood of the Eucharist.[42] The Eucharistic symbolism of the side wound is key for understanding how the mystical transformation of Francis was perceived and thus the significance of the framing of the *camoscio* relic.

One expression of the Eucharistic symbolism of Christ's side wound was the theme of *effusius sanguis*, common in 15th and 16th century iconography, in which blood pouring from Christ's side wound was caught in chalices held by angels. It sometimes served to promote the doctrine of transubstantiation of both species, bread and wine. A clear example is found

Figure 9

in a painting by Benvenuto di Giovanni (ca. 1518) in which the Resurrected Christ fills the chalice at his feet with blood issuing from the side wound (fig. 10, opposite). The effusion of blood pierces through the host, which also appears to bleed into the chalice.

Carlo Crivelli painted a version of the *effusius sanguis* in the 15th century in which the blood from Christ's side is caught in a chalice held by Francis (See fig 11, page 90). Francis is shown kneeling before the Resurrected Christ, who stands before him, the same height as the Tau-shaped cross he is holding, with all the instruments of the Passion on it. Francis is directly facing Christ, and his right hand is positioned to mirror Christ's, as though it revealed the other side of Christ's wound. The chalice Francis holds fills with Christ's blood and seems to symbolize the wounds of his stigmata, which Fausto Zerboni (1641) referred to as "the bitter chalice of wounds in the remains of the body of San Francesco."[43]

The transubstantiated host that "bleeds" into the chalice in Benvenuto di Giovanni's painting suggests that every consecrated host is a miraculous host. Every host can erupt and bleed or turn to flesh like the miraculous hosts in tales of priests with insufficient faith. The fleshy, bleeding hosts of the Eucharistic miracles made the invisible reality of Transubstantiation visible, transforming doubt into faith. This concept, urgently present throughout the medieval period, is the link between the stigmatization of Francis and, for instance, the *Crucifix with St. Francis* by the Master of the San Quirico Cross (refer back to fig. 8) and the Eucharistic framing of Francis stigmatized, blessed and in pain; Francis stigmatized and anointed, host and chalice, receiving the blood of Christ; Francis's side wound stretched open and consecrated, a miraculous host.

The notion of Francis's wounds making the mystery of the Eucharist visible–hinted at in the iconography of the thirteenth through seventeenth centuries and symbolically accomplished with the *camoscio* reliquary of 1602–is explicitly expounded in a sermon delivered in 1672 in the church of the Confraternity of the Stigmata in Rome. In *Sermone delle stimmate di S. Francesco*, the Spanish Jesuit Antonio Vieira tries to explain Christ's purpose, the divine plan, behind the "re-imprinting" of His Passion first in the Eucharist and then in Francis, in the form of stigmata. In both cases, Vieira says, Christ sought to distill the original wounds of their flaws. He is emphatic that on Calvary and in the

Figure 10

Eucharist, the mystery is the same, the Passion is the same, the death is the same; only the ministers are different. The flaws of the Sacrifice on Calvary, Vieira insists, were not in the original wounds, but in their imprinters. On Calvary, ministers of hatred had imprinted on Love; Love stretched out its arms, hatred lifted up the hammers, Love opened its hands, hatred drove in the nails. As a result, according to Vieira, in the original wounds divine charity became mingled with hatred, mercy with injustice, and sacrifice with sacrilege. This flaw, Vieira says, was eliminated in the Eucharist in which the priest acts with reverence. Therefore, Vieira concludes that Christ purified in the Sacrament the villainy of Calvary, correcting in this Second Passion the flaws of the first.

Figure 11

As he leads up to the reason the Sacrifice on Calvary was "re-imprinted" in Francis, Vieira explains that though the consecration of the host during the Mass was done with reverence, it was not necessarily pure. The priest, like the Apostle Thomas who needed to touch Christ's wounds before believing it was Christ, could be plagued with doubt. It was to eliminate this final flaw that Christ robed himself as a Seraph and "re-imprinted" his wounds on Francis:

> This was the manner adopted by Christ when He himself imprinted His wounds in Francis for the second time. In the Sacrament He re-imprinted His Passion, in Francis He consecrated [made a sacrament of] His wounds . . .; in the Sacrament He hid the mystery of Faith; in Francis He made visible the mystery of Charity. As Christ with His Love is the ministrant in the consecration of the Sacrament, Christ and His Love was likewise the craftsman in imprinting His wounds, so that having purified in Francis the villainy of Calvary His wounds endured, entirely sacred, wholly beautiful and wholly loveable.[44]

Vieira equates stigmatization with transubstantiation in which Christ unveiled the mystery hidden in the Eucharist. The stigmatization was an act in which Christ, without the intermediary of the priest, consecrated his own wounds on Francis's body, making "visible the mystery of charity." Vieira then asks forgiveness of the Sacrament, because he cannot help but notice an advantage in the impression of the wounds in Francis. What was the advantage? In the stigmata, Christ Himself was the sole minister, who made the invisible Sacrament of the Eucharist visible. Vieira likens Francis's stigmatized body to a visible sacrament, as though he had been transformed into a living Eucharist.

In a statement that is astoundingly bold, Vieira suggests that the stigmatized Francis not only surpasses the Eucharist, but his side wound surpasses the side wound of Christ. This is because unlike Christ, Francis felt the pain of the side wound.

> Here is the spear, the wound and the transferred pain of Francis . . . .And this living man . . . will endure the pain of the spear . . . .Christ's was one, but three were the blows: one in Christ, one in Mary and the third in Francis. That of Christ wounded the body but not the spirit; that of Mary wounded the spirit but not the body; that of Francis wounded the body and spirit together. Christ received the blow but did not feel the pain. Mary felt the pain but did not receive the blow. Francis received and felt the blow and he felt the pain. That is why Francis's side oozed blood every Friday. Only blood, not blood and water as in Christ's side, because blood drawn with pain is pure blood, it is not watered down.[45]

Vieira goes so far as to suggest that the pain of stigmatization surpassed that of the Passion since Francis endured "the pain of the spear" and, in addition, the pain of the side wound which Christ was spared was transferred to him who "received and felt the blow and he felt the pain."

In the Greek liturgy of the Mass the host was at one time distributed with a spear-shaped paten, while the priest repeated the words from John's Gospel, "one of the soldiers pierced his side with a spear, and at once blood and water came out."[46] Similarly, the Eucharistic monstrance offers the *camoscio*, the relic described "as if pierced with a lance" to the gaze of the devotee as though it were a host that had turned to flesh, like the miraculous host in Lanciano.[47] It presents Francis's body for veneration in a kind of "static '*elevatio.*'"[48] In a letter to the clergy, Francis wrote that the Eucharist "cannot be His Body without first being consecrated by word. For we have and see nothing bodily of the Most High in this world except His Body and Blood. . . ."[49] Francis would undoubtedly have been shocked to see his own body presented as consecrated, framed as a miraculous host, a relic of the Body of Christ.

Using imagery that, wittingly or unwittingly, evokes the *camoscio* in its solar monstrance, Vieira extols the devotional power the stigmata has to:

> thaw a world grown cold and to rekindle human hearts, ... rays emanating from the body of the Sun do not burn, while reflected in a mirror they ignite. Thus it was. Christ is the sun, Francis the mirror, the wounds the rays, His love the fire and our hearts the inflammable matter.[50]

This could as easily be a description of the devotional impact of the *camoscio* relic. In the Eucharistic monstrance, the side wound of Francis is at once conflated with the side wound of Christ and elevated to the status of a consecrated host. At the same time, it remains distinct from Christ's wound, more propitious for being miraculous, more touching for being human, more exemplary for being within our reach.

Though the relic of the *camoscio* has few textual sources, its evocative form and the symbolic richness of its framing make it visually eloquent, like Francis's wounds themselves. Thomas of Celano wrote:

> ... words would be unable to express such marvels,
> soiled as they are by cheap and everyday things.
> For this reason perhaps
> it had to appear in the flesh,
> since it could not be explained in words.
> Therefore,
> let silence speak, where word falls short,
> for symbol cries out as well, where sign falls short.
> This alone intimates to human ears
> what is not entirely clear:
> why that sacrament appeared in the saint.[51]

Mystical union has always defied verbal expression. In the case of Francis, mystery is layered with paradox: mystical union usually refers to the soul's purification from the body and absorption into Christ, but the union on Mount La Verna was seen to have occurred in the body of Francis, and the stigmatization of Francis was compared to the mystical transformation of the host into the body of Christ. The distance between Francis's and Christ's body was collapsed. Just as

Francis resided in Christ's wound, the mystery of Christ lived in the body of Francis. The *camoscio* relic in its monstrance captures the paradox of the mystical experience it embodies. The physical object is used to amplify a silence, the emptiness at its centre. It offers the devotee an invitation to penetrate the side wound of Francis and follow him into the mystery of the Passion of Christ. Therefore, let silence speak.

Notes

[1] This article is adapted from my doctoral thesis, in which I examine devotional practices and reflections around the contact relics and blood relics of the stigmata of St. Francis. See Carla Salvati, *The Relics of the Stigmata of St. Francis of Assisi*, Ph.D. Thesis, Department of Religion, Concordia University, Montreal (2005). I am greatly indebted to Rose Ftaya for her invaluable suggestions and careful editing of this article. I am also indebted to Thea Pawlikowska for her assistance with the Italian translations and Joseph Salvati for his ever-patient technical assistance.

[2] Thomas of Celano, The Remembrance of the Desire of a Soul (hereafter referred to as 2C), Second Book, CLIII, in *Francis of Assisi: Early Documents* vol. 2, *The Founder*, eds. R.J. Armstrong, J.A.W. Hellmann and W.J. Short (New York: New City Press, 2000), 376. This volume is hereafter referred to as *FAED* 2 with page number.

[3] The *camoscio* is on display at the Relic Museum of the Lower Church of the Basilica of St. Francis in Assisi.

[4] On the pessimism that pervaded Europe after the Black Death, see M. Meiss, *Painting in Florence and Siena after the Black Death, The Arts, Religion and Society in the Mid-Fourteenth Century* (Princeton: Princeton University Press, 1951).

[5] See M. Rubin, *Corpus Christi: The Eucharist in Late Medieval Culture* (Cambridge: Cambridge University Press, 1991), 394: "Masses dedicated to the wounds first appear from the early fourteenth century in sections of votive masses in missals, and in private books of prayer, often accompanied by appropriate pictures of open gashes. Interest in the wounds developed into a special devotion; and further into a feast with its mass *Humiliavit* and indulgences in the fourteenth century." For more examples see Dom Louis Gougaud, *Dévotions et Pratiques Ascétiques du Moyen Age* (Paris: Desclée de Brouwer, 1925), 87ff.

[6] Gougaud, *Dévotions et Pratiques*, 80. Original reads: "*C'est de la stigmatization de l'Alverne, 'le grand miracle'. . . que date véritablement l'avènement triomphal des cinq plaies dans la vénération du moyen age.*"

[7] Quoted in O. Schmucki, *The Stigmata of St. Francis of Assisi: A Critical Investigation in the Light of Thirteenth-Century Sources* (St. Bonaventure, NY: The Franciscan Institute, 1991), 223, note 14. Schmucki gives other sources on the care of the wounds, see the anonymous *Vita Fratris Leonis*, in *Analecta Francescana* 3: 65-74: "How only he touched the wounds of Blessed Francis" (68); Bartholomew of Pisa, *De Conformitate vitae beati Francisci ad vitam Domini Jesu* (1385-90), Fructus XXXI (Lib III Fruct III), *Analecta Francescana* 4 (1912): 189-90: "Br. Leo very frequently saw these Stigmata, because he placed dressings between the nails and

the flesh every day except Friday, and changed the wound in the side. In fact, Blessed Francis many times exposed his hands to Br. Leo's gaze and when Br. Leo looked at them, he experienced the greatest consolation."

[8] *Actus Beati Francisci et Sociorum Eius*, Consideration 3, quoted in Schmucki, 223, note 14.

[9] This is a recurring motif in descriptions of the stigmata. For instance, Thomas of Celano tells us that Francis wore woolen socks to hide the wounds on his feet, ". . . placing a piece of leather over the wounds to soften the wool's roughness." 2C, Second Book, XCVIII. See *FAED 2*, 335.

[10] The entry is found in Inventory #41 of the *Inventari alfabetici della basilica e sacristia di S. Francesco, ordinati dal P. Filippo Gesualdo, Generale O.F.M. nell' 1600, integrati fino al 1609*; registro 205, 101: "*Un tabernacolo d'argento nel quale vi è una scritta fatta per mano di S. Francesco qual mandò a frà Leone: in cima ci sono delle pezze con [le quale] le gli asciuttava le sue piaghe.*" (A silver tabernacle in which is a note in Saint Francis's hand, which he sent to Brother Leo: on top of which are pieces of cloth with which he dried his wounds.)

[11] The casket, with the stigmata in silver relief on the cover, was donated to the Bishop of Assisi in 1596 by Charles Borromeo. The original note accom-panying the donation is preserved in the *Archivio vescovile di Assisi*, Scans. IV, vol. 34, c.118. I am very grateful to Sister Chiara Anastasia Hill of the Proto-Monastery of St. Clare in Assisi for sharing her knowledge of this and other historical sources of the *impiastro* and for allowing me to see and photograph the relic.

[12] Bartolomew of Pisa, *De Conformitate*, 410: "*Beata Clara vidit stigmata beati Francisci dum viveret et vulneri laterali emplastrum quoddam ipsa fecit, ut hodie (adhuc) ostenditur in monasterio Sanctae Clarae de Assisio.*" According to Bonaventure, while a number of brothers saw Francis's wounds while he was still alive, Clare only saw them after his death. See his *Major Legend of St. Francis*, hereafter referred to as LMj, Chapter 13, in *FAED* 2, 636.

[13] Luke Wadding, *Annales Minorum ad annum 1224*, n. 18, t. II (Quaracchi: Collegio S. Bonaventura, 1931), 106: *In Ecclesia sancti Georgii Clarissarum Assisii vidi adhuc servari quoddam genus cataplasmatis, seu emplastri // vulgo italico antiquo "camocium" dictum, quod ad leniendum lateralis plagae dolorem, et sanguinem retinendum Viro sancto fecit virgo sanctissima Clara.* The relic is also mentioned in *La Franceschina: testo volgare Umbro del secolo XV*, ed. N. Cavanna (Florence: Olschki, 1931), chapter 8: (. . . she made for the side wound a kind of poultice which is exposed in the monastery of St. Clare in Assisi). Antonio Daza in *Descrizione delle stimmate del nostro Serafico Padre San Francesco* (Florence: Appresso I Giunti, 1619), 120, seems to be describing either the *impiastro* or the *camoscio* when he writes: "*La Benedetta S. Chiara vivendo il nostro Padre San Francesco meritò vedere le piaghe de'piedi, e delle mani, e per quella del costato fece di sua propria mano uno incerato, ò socrocio, per conservarla più guardata, e più difesa dall'asprezza dell'habito: il quale si conserva, e si mostra, come pietosa reliquia nel Convento di S. Chiara d'Ascesi*" (While our Father Francis was still alive, the Blessed St. Clare was worthy to see the wounds in his feet and in his hands. For the side wound she herself made an oilcloth or (*socrocio?*) to hide it and protect it against the coarseness of the habit. This is preserved and shown as a holy relic in the convent of St. Clare in Assisi). [Unless otherwise indicated all translations are mine].

[14] This inventory was published by Michele Faloci-Pulignani, in "Le Sacre Reliquie della Basilica di San Francesco in Assisi nel secolo XIV," *Miscellanea Francescana* I (1901): 145-50.

[15] Pulignani, 146-47.

[16] Pulignani, 149.

[17] Bonaventure Mariangeli, "Il Reliquario della 'Pelle di Camoscio,'" *Miscellanea Francescana* XVII (1916): 95. On p. 94 Mariangeli comments that at first glance the tear has the appearance of a wound.

[18] Quoted in Schmucki, 264.

[19] Thomas of Celano, *Treatise on the Miracles of Saint Francis*, Chapter 2, in *FAED* 2. See also Bonaventure, LMj Chapter 13: "Also his right side, as if pierced with a lance, was marked with a red wound from which his sacred blood often flowed, moistening his tunic and underwear."

[20] See G. Ciofi, *Santuarii della Serafica Città d'Assisi, con la Notizia de Corpi Santi, Reliquie insigni, e memorie, ch'ivi si conservano* (Ancona, 1664), 23-24: "*Una Stella d'Argento con una Pezza di camoscio quale S. Francesco portava alla Sacra Piaga del Costato, che S. Chiara gli la medicava, con il Sangue, con l'impiastro, e impressione della Piaga, la quale con solenne Processione si porta per la Città la festa delle Sacre Stimati alli 17 del mese di Settembre.*"

[21] See L. Gougaud, "La Prière dite de Charlemagne," *Revue d'Histoire ecclésiastique* XX (1924): 211-38.

[22] Gougaud, "La Priere," 223: "*Le rouleau Harl T ii, qui mesure 1 m22 de long sur 9 cm de large, contient, outré la mesure du corps du Christ représentée par une croix en forme de Tau . . . la mesure de la plaie du coté droit du Sauveur, laquelle est représentée par un losange peint en rouge, long de 7 cm.*"

[23] See W. Sparrow Simpson, "On the Measure of the Wound in the Side of the Redeemer," *The Journal of the British Archaeological Association* (December, 1874), 359.

[24] See L.M.J. Delaisée, J. Marrow and J. de Wit, *Illuminated Manuscripts* (Fribourg: Office of the Livre, 1977), 469. For an in-depth analysis of devotion to the measurements of the side wound of Christ, see D. S. Areford, "The Passion Measured: A Late-Medieval Diagram of the Body of Christ," in *The Broken Body, Passion Devotion in Late-Medieval Culture* (Groningen: Egbert Forsten, 1998), especially 213: ". . . the woodcut employs these measurements in order to establish both a spatial and a devotional precision, exemplifying a late-medieval tension between the rendering of symbolic space and 'real' space." On the side wound of Christ and gender, see C. Bynum, *Jesus as Mother: Studies in the Spirituality of the High Middle Ages* (Berkeley: University of California Press, 1982), 120-23. See also F. Lewis, "The Wound in Christ's side and the Instruments of the Passion: Gendered Experience and Response," in *Women and the Book: Assessing the Visual Evidence* (Toronto: University of Toronto Press, 1996), 204-23. On the evolution of the devotion to the Sacred Heart from the devotion to the side wound see, M.V. Bernadot, "Le développement historique de la dévotion au Sacré-Cœur," *La vie spirituelle* II (1920): 193-215.

[25] See Gougaud, *Dévotions et Pratiques*, 100: "*Il arrive aussi que cette forme soit indiquée, sur les estampes du XVe siècle, par une simple découpure pratiquée dans le papier.*"

[26] The tear in the camoscio is approximately 4 cm. wide.

²⁷From "The Stigmata of St. Francis" from a Franciscan manuscript breviary (15th-16th centuries). See *FAED 3, The Prophet*, eds. R.J. Armstrong, J.A.W. Hellmann, and W.J. Short (New York: New City Press, 2001), 669: "Jesus, You changed the weeping of Francis sweetly, when You tore the sack of flesh in that five-fold way. The heart of Francis is pierced with loving arrows, the piercing showing forth in his flesh with beautiful wounds." Herafter, FAED 3 with page number.

²⁸LMj, Chapter 13. See *FAED 2*, 630-39.

²⁹See Mariangeli, 92. In an Inventory from 1473, the *camoscio* was in a casket of gilt bronze, *Item unum tabernaculum de ramine inauratum in quo est camussium quod sanctus Franciscus portavit super vulnus laterale*, (Here is a tabernacle [shrine] of gilt bronze in which is the chamois that St. Francis wore on the side wound), Mariangeli, 93. A new reliquary was commissioned for the *camoscio* in 1479. The original contract begins, "Wishing for the honour and glory of our Patriarch St. Francis, to make a shrine that is fitting and worthy for the *camoscio* that St. Francis placed on the side wound. . . ." (*Volendo per honore et gloria del patriarca San Francesco fare uno tabernacolo condecente e degno dove se allochi el camoscio quale san Francesco portava alla piaga del costato. . .*). The contract is published in G. Fratini, *Storia della Basilica e del Convento di S. Francesco in Assisi* (Prato: Raineri Guasti, 1882), 279-81. We do not know whether this reliquary was ever made, but records exist of the silver objects collected to be melted down to provide the silver for it. They are listed in the inventory of the Basilica of the Sacro Convento in Assisi from 1473, published in F. Pennacchi, "I Piu Antichi Inventari della Sacristia del sacro convento di Assisi-Bibli Com. Di Assisi, cod. 337," *Archivum Franciscanum Historicum* (1914): 294-312.

³⁰See T. Verdon, "Il 'pane vivo': la teologia, le immagini, il percorso," *Panis Vivus* (Siena: Protagon, 1994), 45. See also E. Rupin, *L'oeuvre de Limoges* (Paris, 1890), 504, "*Celle de soleil, indiquant une forme spéciale, date de l'epoque a laquelle les orfèvres donnèrent au contour de l'hostie l'apparence de cet aster projetant des rayons alternativement droits et flamboyants; on la trouve employée pour la première fois dans l'Inventaire du Trésor de la Sainte-Chapelle de Bourges dresse en 1405.*" See also M. Andrieu "Aux origines du culte du Saint-Sacrement, reliquaires et monstrances eucharistiques," *Analecta Bollandina* 68 (1950): 397-418.

³¹See Verdon, 45. For a brief summary of the cult of the tablet of St. Bernardino see "Le trigramme *IHS* et le culte du Nom de Jésus," of A. Vauchez, in *Histoire des saints et de la sainteté chrétienne* (Paris: Beauchesne, 1986), Tome VII, 80.

³²On the Arezzo Crucifix see Georges Didi-Huberman, "Un Sang D'images," *Nouvelle Revue de Psychanalyse* 32 (1985): 137, which reads: "*. . . les filets de sang christique traversent le corps du saint aux lieux mêmes de sa stigmatisation . . . le sang coule aussi de part et d'autre de son pied, comme s'il le transperçait, comme si François lui-même saignait du sang du Christ. . . .*"

³³See Bonaventure, *The Tree of Life*, trans. E. Cousins (New York: Paulist Press, 1978), Eighth Fruit, for his evocation of Christ anointing his own body with his blood: "Christ the Lord was stained with his own blood, which flowed profusely: first from the bloody sweat, then from the lashes and the thorns, then from the nails and finally from the lance. So that with God there might be plenteous redemption, he wore a priestly robe of red; his apparel was truly red and his garments like those of the wine presser." See W. R. Cook, *Images of St. Francis of Assisi in Painting, Stone and Glass from the Earliest Images to ca. 1320* (Florence: Olschki, 1999), 145. Cook

comments that the San Quirico *Crucifix with St. Francis* "is the only known image of Francis in a medallion on a cross. He is in some ways quite separated from the crucifixion, yet he is experiencing it through the blood. This painting is another example of a work including Francis that was probably not commissioned by or for the friars and that downplays his stigmata."

[34]Bonaventure, *Holiness of Life (De Perfectione Vitae ad Sorores)*, trans. L. Costello (St. Louis: Herder, 1923), 63.

[35]Bonaventure, *Holiness of Life*, 63.

[36]Daza, *Descrizione delle stimmate*, 53-54. The passage reads: "*La prima volta, che'l nostro Padre S. Francesco arrivò à questo Monte, andando dentro à più scoscesi luoghi, per trovarvi un luogo più solitario per darsi all'orazione, vedde alcune pietre rotte con assai grandi aperture, e fra l'altre una d'assai notabile grandezza, ch'era come tagliata, e divisa dall'altre, e quasi in aria, sostentata per una parte sola, sopra una picciola pietra, cosa, che dette molto da pensare al Santo, parendogli cosa impossibile da farsi per industria humana; per esser in parte tanto remota, & appartata, dove à pena già mai arrivò persona, ne v'habitò fino all'hora. Al fine entrò il Santo nella Concavità & apertura di questa pietra, . . . supplicando nostro Signore, che gli desse ad intendere la causa di si gran maraviglia. . . . Finì il Santo la sua oratione, e gl'apparve un'Angiolo, e gli disse*. Francesco, questa Pietra che vedi, con molte altre, che sono in questo Monte, s'apersero, e si spezzorono nella morte del nostro Signore Gesù Cristo, *e da all'hora in poi cominciò à tenere in più veneratione questo santo luogo, e andarvi molte volte per gl'esercitij dell'oratione, e della penitenza . . . .*" Emphasis (non-italics) mine.

[37]Daza, 52, *Descrizione delle stimmate*: "*Questo Sacro Monte, (che si può chiamare quasi un'altro mistico Calvario per le gran maraviglie, ch'oprò Iddio in esso)*."

[38]Bonaventure, *Tree of Life*, Eighth Fruit.

[39]*The Coming of the Friars Minor to England and Germany Being the Chronicles of Brother Thomas of Eccleston and Brother Jordan of Giano*, trans. E. Gurney-Salter (London: J.M. Dent, 1926),109-10.

[40]*La Franceschina*, 443-44. The passage reads: "*. . . Quisto frate perserverò longo tempo in oratione, pregando sempre Yhesu Christo che li piacesse mostrargli santo Francesco. Et stando una sera in uno certo loco diserto in oratione, vidde uno choro de santi passare per la selva a lato ad esso, et domandò lui chi fosse. Li fo dicto che era lo choro de li confessori, lo quale guidavano santo Augustino et santo Gregorio dottori santi. Et domandando quisto frate si c'era intra loro santo Francesco, li fo resposto de no. Et quillo dixe: 'Andate nel nome di Dio.' Anche venne el secondo choro piu splendido; et domandando chi era, respuse che era lo choro de li santi martiri, et guidavanlo santo Stephano et santo Lorenzo. Et domandando si c'era santo Francesco intra loro, li fo resposto de no. Dixe: 'Andate nel nome de Dio'. Venne el terzo choro che era più splendente che li primi, che era de li santi Apostoli; et domandando si c'era intra loro santo Francesco, li fo detto de no. Dixe: 'Andate nel nome de Dio'. Venne un altro choro bellissimo che era de le sante Vergene, nel quale era la gloriosa Vergene Maria matre del Salvatore. Et similemente domandando si c'era santo Francesco intra loro, li fo ditto de no. Dixe el frate: 'Andate nel nome de Dio'. Ultimamente venne el choro de l'altri santi molto più splendente, nel quale era Christo co li santi Angeli, et lo frate domandò si lì era santo Francesco. Et allora santo Michele Arcangelo sorrise, et co la faccia alegra dixe al Signore che andava innante: 'O, Signore, questo frate desidera de vedere santo Francesco: si piace a la vostra benignità, prego gli li mostriate.' Dixe lo Signore: 'Me piace; lo vega.' Et alzò lo Signore lo braccio deritto; et levandolo sù, santo Francesco uscì fore de la piaga laterale del*

nostro Signore Yhesu Christo. Et vedendo quello frate santo Francesco, subito el suo core fo repieno de gaudio et consolatione, et curre ad esso. Al quale dixe santo Francesco: 'O cativello, que fai tu? Tu ài qui el tuo Signore Yhesu Christo . . . et gettossi a li piedi de Yhesu Christo, recognoscendo la sua colpa.'" This story was first recounted in Bartolomew of Pisa's *De Conformitate*.

[41] The engraving by Bernard Picart is from the 1734 French edition of the *Alcoran* by Erasmus, first published in 1542, entitled *L'Alcoran des Cordeliers tant en Latin qu'en François*. . . .The caption for the illustration reads "*St. François apparoit à un des frères sortant du côté de notre Seigneur, tenant à la main l'Etendart de la Croix.*" I owe a debt of gratitude to Father Servus Gieben, OFM Cap., for pointing out this illustration to me.

[42] See St. Augustine, *Tractates on the Gospel of John*, trans. J.W. Rettig (Washington, DC: Catholic University Press, 1988-95), tractate 120: "the Evangelist used a wide awake word so that he did not say, 'pierced his side' or 'wounded' or anything else, but 'opened', so that there, in a manner of speaking, the door of life was thrown open from which the mystical rites [*sacramenta*] of the Church flowed." Or more dramatically, Bonaventure: "the divine plan permitted that one of the soldiers should pierce open his sacred side with a lance. While blood mixed with water flowed, the price of our salvation was poured forth, which gushing from the secret fountain of the heart gave power to the sacraments of the Church, to confer the life of grace . . . ." (*Tree of Life*, Eighth Fruit).

[43] See Fausto Zerboni, *Ragionamento delle Sacre Stimate di S. Francesco* (Rome, 1641), 7: "*l'amaro calice delle piaghe nel sacco del corpo di Francesco.*"

[44] Antonio Vieira, *Sermone delle Stimmate di S. Francesco* (Rome, 1672), 10: *Tal fù lo stile che osservò Cristo nella seconda stampa delle sue piaghe imprimendole per se stesso in Francesco. Nel sacramento ristampò la sua passione, in Francesco sacramentò le sue piaghe: nel Sacramento pose la passione invisibile; in Francesco fece il Sacramento visibile: nel Sacramento occultò il misterio della fede; in Francesco manifestò il misterio della Carità: E come nella consecratione del Sacramento Cristo, e'l suo Amore è'l ministro; così nella impressione delle piaghe Cristo altresì, e'l suo Amore fù l'artefice: accioche, purificata in Francesco la malvagità del Calvario, rimanessero le sue piaghe e di ogni parte sante, e di ogni parte belle, e di ogni parte amabili.*"

[45] Vieira, *Sermone delle Stimmate* 20-22.

[46] See *Spiegazione dell'Apertura del costato di Nostro Signor Gesù Cristo* (Venezia, 1781), 47. This work by an anonymous author was translated from the French version of Duguet into Italian by Antonio Pezzano.

[47] See David Sox, *Relics and Shrines* (London and Boston: Allen and Unwin, 1985), chapter 9, on the Eucharistic miracle of Lanciano. The miracle of Lanciano is the earliest of the Eucharistic miracles. Legend dates the miracle to the 8th century when the doubts of a priest resulted in the host turning to flesh and the wine to blood. Both relics continue to be shown in an eighteenth-century monstrance in the Franciscan church in Lanciano in the Abruzzi region of Italy.

[48] See G.J.C. Snoek, *Medieval Piety from Relics to the Eucharist: A Process of Mutual Interaction* (Leiden/New York: Brill, 1995), 62. "The introduction of the procession on the feast of *Corpus Christi* led to 'exposition,' a kind of static, consisting of placing the Eucharistic bread on or above the altar. . . ."

⁴⁹See "Exhortations to the Clergy," *FAED* 1, 52.
⁵⁰Vieira, 25. The passage reads: *"Dunque per riscaldar la freddezza del mondo e per infiammar e accender i cuori humani, non è molto che siano più efficaci, o veramente più proportionate, le piaghe di Cristo in Francesco, che nell'istesso Cristo. I raggi che vibrati dal corpo del Sole non accendono, passati per uno specchio sveglian fuoco. Così fù. Cristo e il Sole, Francesco lo specchio, le piaghe i raggi, il suo amore il fuoco, e la materia i cuori nostri."*
⁵¹2C, Second Book, CLIV, *FAED* 2, 377.

LIST OF FIGURES

Figure 1: Reliquary of the *camoscio* (1602), Basilica of St. Francis in Assisi. Photo: Pianeta Immagine, Rome. Reprint permission requested.

Figure 2: Reliquary of the *impiastro* (1596), Monastery of St. Clare. Photo by author. Used in dissertation.

Figure 3: *Measure of the Wound in the Side of the Lord*. Book of Hours, (15th c.). Reproduced from W. Sparrow Simpson, "On the Measure of the Wound in the Side of the Redeemer," *The Journal of the British Archaeological Association* (December, 1874).

Figure 4: *Angels with Reliquary of Side Wound*. Book of Hours, (15th c.). Reproduced from: L.M.J. Delaissé, J. Marrow and J. de Wit, *Illuminated Manuscripts* (Fribourg: Office du Livre, 1977).

Figure 5: Close-up *camoscio* relic. Used in dissertation.

Figure 6: *San Bernardino of Siena* (detail), by Sano di Pietro, (15th c.), Museum of the Abruzzi, L'Aquila. Reproduced from: *Histoire des saints et de la sainteté chrétienne*, tome 7, ed. A. Vauchez (Paris: Hachette, 1986). Used in dissertation.

Figure 7: *Crucifix with St. Francis*, Master of the San Quirico Cross, (ca.1315), Osteria Nuova, San Quirico a Ruballa. Reproduced with author's permission from: W. R. Cook, *Images of St. Francis of Assisi in Painting, Stone and Glass from the Earliest Images to ca. 1320* (Florence: L.S. Olschki, 1999).

Figure 8: Detail, figure 7.

Figure 9: *St. Francis in the Side Wound of Christ*. Engraving, (1734). Reproduced from A. Erasmus, *L'Alcoran des Cordeliers tant en Latin qu'en Francois...* (1734 edition).

Figure 10: *The Blood of the Redeemer*, Benvenuto di Giovanni (15th c.). From *Panis Vivus: Arredi e testimonianze figurative del culto eucaristico dal VI al XIX secolo*, Cecilia Alessi and Laura Martini (Siena: Protagon, 1994). This was a catalogue for use in connection witht the XXIInd Eucharisitc Congress held in Siena in 1994.

Figure 11: *St. Francis of Assisi*, Carlo Crivelli (1468). Photo: Museo Poldi-Pezzoli, Milano. Permission requested by author.

Figure 1: *Reliquary of the camoscio (1602)*
Basilica of St. Francis in Assisi.
Photo: Pianeta Immagine, Rome. Permission requested.

Figure 2: *Reliquary of the impiastro (1596), Monastery of St. Clare, Assisi.* Photo by author.

Figure 3: Measure of the Wound in the Side of the Lord. *Book of Hours (15th c.).* Reproduced from: W. Sparrow Simpson, "On the Measure of the Wound in the Side of the Redeemer," 1874.

Figure 4: Angels with Reliquary of Side Wound. *Book of Hours (15th c.).* Reproduced from: *L.M.J. Delaisée, J. Marrow and J.de Wit,* Illuminated Manuscripts. *Permission obtained by Carla Salvati.*

Figure 5: *Close-up of the camoscio relic.*

Figure 6:
San Bernardino of Siena *(detail)*, *Sano di Pietro, (15th c.), Museum of the Abruzzi, l'Aquila. Reproduced from* Histoire des saints et de la sainteté chrétienne, *vol. 7. Permission, Carla Salvati.*

Figure 7:
Crucifix with St. Francis, *Master of the San Quirico Cross, (ca.1315), Osteria Nuova, San Quirico a Ruballa. Reproduced from W. R. Cook*, Images of St. Francis of Assisi in Painting, Stone and Glass from the Earliest Images to ca. 1320. *With permission of W.R. Cook.*

Figure 8:
Detail, figure 7.

Figure 9:
St. Francis in the side wound of Christ. *Engraving, (1734). Reproduced from: A. Erasmus, L'Alcoran des Cordeliers tant en Latin qu'en Francois . . . (1734 edition). Permission: Carla Salvati.*

Figure 10:
The Blood of the Redeemer, *Benvenuto di Giovanni (15th c.). Reproduced from:* Panis Vivus: Arredi e testimonianze figurative del culto eucaristico dal VI al XIX secolo. *Permission, Carla Salvati.*

Figure 11: St. Francis of Assisi. *Carlo Crivelli (1468). Photo: Museo Poldi-Pezzoli, Milano. Permission, Carla Salvati.*